Professional Development Management File
Series Editor: Dr Harry Tolley

Developing
as a
Teacher of
History

Julian Stern

Brunel University

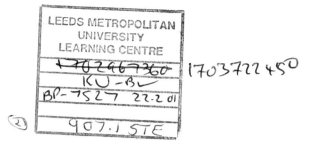
© Julian Stern 1999

ISBN 1 899857 18 4

First published 1999 by

Chris Kington Publishing

27 Rathmore Road
Cambridge CB1 7AB

British Library cataloguing in publication data. A catalogue record for this book is available from the British Library.

Printed in the United Kingdom by York Publishing Services,
64 Hallfield Road, Layerthorpe, York YO3 7XQ

CONTENTS

Introduction   5

    Aims of this book   5

    Using this book   5

*1: From learner-teacher
to teacher-learner*   7

    Evidence of standards & competences in training
    courses and in school   7

    Evidence of reflective practice: your attitude to
    professional development   8

    Your place in the learning organisation: life is an
    action research project   22

*2: From your history to
you're history*   23

    Justifying history   23

    History in the whole curriculum: humanities and
    beyond   26

    Doing, being, and learning about history: does it
    make a difference how much I know?   26

3: Planning history   29

    Time marches on: planning for chronology   30

    Periodic tables: planning for content   31

    Digging for victory: planning for using evidence   33

    Get it in perspective: planning for dealing with
    different viewpoints   33

    Giving it fizz: planning for engagement   35

*4: Differentiation in history: from
proficient teacher to advanced
skills teacher*   37

    Pedagogy for a purpose   37

    The differentiated department: making the
    most of diversity, through mutual observation and
    support   38

    Flexible learning: avoiding the two-faced teacher   41

    DART activities: core experiences, differentiated work   42

    Homework: grabbing hold of the world and
    making it make sense for you   43

5: Resources in history   47

    Texts and textbooks as teachers and as sources:
    class sets, book boxes, and libraries   47

    Stories, songs and pictures: narrative drive and
    imaginative leaps   48

    Information and communication technology and
    history: byting back   50

    Wonderful worksheets   51

    People as sources: pupils, teachers, families, and
    beyond   53

    Places as sources: using environments, starting with
    the classroom   54

    Objects as sources: using artefacts   57

    Making resource banks   59

6: Assessment   63

    Why assess?   63

    Understanding levels and understanding progress   66

    Making a mark: short term assessment   68

    Going public: long term assessment and reporting   69

    Self-assessment: from pupils to teachers   73

7: Making history matter   79

    History and personal, social, moral, spiritual and
    cultural development   79

    History as communication   82

    Access to history: equal opportunities and special
    needs   83

    History and policy in department and school   85

8: Professional development in history   87

    What is expertise in history teaching?   87

    From managing pupils to managing teachers:
    careering through history   88

    Managing yourself: having the confidence to
    carry on learning, reflecting, and action planning   91

*Bibliography: sourcebooks for
development*   93

Index   103

AUTHOR'S PREFACE

Going around toy shops, I am struck by the division often made between 'toys' and the hushed corner containing 'educational toys'. The puzzle is that children learn from all the toys they play with, so why call only a small group of toys 'educational'? There is a similar puzzle regarding teacher development. INSET and other formal systems of professional development are often shoved into a 'hushed corner' of a teacher's work. Yet teachers develop all the time, whether or not they attend courses. This book, for developing teachers of history, is based on the belief that teachers inevitably develop, that they want to be better than they are, and that 'development' should not be separated from, or seen as an optional addition to, the everyday work of the teacher. The toys are all jumbled up. I hope the book will be used in that spirit.

Of those who take a similar approach to teacher development, I'd particularly like to acknowledge the work of Jean Jones and of Terry Haydn. Only one of these (Terry) is a historian, and I recommend that all developing history teachers seek inspiration, in a similar way, from within and beyond the world of history. Looking inwards, to history, is an immensely valuable activity; looking outwards, to other disciplines and perspectives, is its essential complement.

This is a book for history teachers, rather than a book of history, and I've tried to model the approach of looking inward, looking outward. That means, inevitably in such a short book, that there will be plenty of gaps. I hope that what remains is still useful. Meanwhile, I'm happy to take full responsibility for all the mistakes in, as well as omissions from, the text. However, I'm too much of a historian to think that any simple cause-effect relationship can be found.

Of those who helped in the production of this book, I'd particularly like to acknowledge the critical and proof-reading help given by Pam Rauchwerger, and the equally constructive critiques offered over many years by pupils, students, and teachers of history.

Julian Stern

July 1998

INTRODUCTION

Aims of this book

When student teachers are finding teacher-training a strain, some bright spark will usually say "Just wait until you see what it's like in your first year of real teaching". Well, this book focuses on the first years in which, having qualified, you are doing paid professional teaching, teaching history, and hoping that you made the right decision. The aim of the book, therefore, is to support the new teacher of history through these early years. Inevitably, new teachers come into the profession with a variety of backgrounds and experiences, from varied training courses and with different academic and work experiences behind them. What the book is not trying to do, however, is to fill in 'training gaps' left by courses, or to be a bare survival guide. Two underlying assumptions are that training (and prior experience and study) has equipped you with sufficient competence, and an appropriate attitude, to begin your career. Of course, student teachers still completing their PGCEs or BEds, and recently qualified teachers (RQTs) are welcome to use this book as a basis for further development.

There are enough common issues raised by new teachers in schools around the country to justify the adoption here of a common approach. Although teachers in different subject areas will have many needs in common (addressed by the generic NQT book in this series), history teachers deserve a book to themselves. History is a subject particularly well suited to helping teachers develop, with its approach stressing the need for evidence, critically examined, and for an appreciation of varied perspectives and interpretations. Even the historian's understanding of chronology and change over time should aid reflection: the new teacher will be contemplating a career just starting out, full of possibilities.

This author's **Learning to Teach** *(Stern, 1995) is an attempt to support the work of all teachers wishing to learn; Capel et al (1997) addresses NQT needs in particular; Tolley (1996e) is the book in the Chris Kington Publishing series for NQTs.*

History departments, too, are special places, and a book aiming to support teachers working within them is most certainly needed. Where history is taught within a humanities faculty, it is worth considering the relationship between history and its companions (usually geography and RE, sometimes sociology, and other subjects). Where history is the specialist subject of a primary teacher, work across subjects is of course inevitable.

Fisher (1998) is the book in this series for geography teachers. A valuable read for any beginning teacher.

A further aim of this book, an aim that the author is tempted to hide from readers other than beginning teachers, is to allow them to help more experienced history teachers. When schools appoint NQTs, they often do so because they think new teachers are easier to 'mould' into the school's (or the department's) ethos. However, they also have in mind the idea that newer teachers are more likely to bring in new practices, and may invigorate the more experienced staff: they may believe in a sort of 'trickle up' theory. An NQT should exploit this, but exploit it with great delicacy, as there is a fine line between being 'refreshing' and being 'arrogant'. Working through this book, with a more senior colleague as a mentor, may allow for that 'trickle up' to take place without causing too much offence.

Frank Lloyd Wright said "From the ground up makes good sense for building. Beware of from the top down". This often applies to the development of teachers, who can (and should) learn most from pupils, and almost as much from new and newish teachers.

On this basis, beginning teachers can negotiate their professional development from a position of some strength. Other books in this series (notably Tolley et al, 1996e p 25) refer to learning contracts. Contracts imply mutual agreements, ideal for any formalisation of professional relationships, and particularly useful where both parties have something to gain from the contract.

Using this book

This book contains:

- **ideas**, mostly in blocks of text;
- **references** for following up ideas, mostly in the margin, in italics;
- **activities**, in the form of text and tables.

There are therefore three strands in the book, running alongside each other. Some readers will wish to spend more time working on one of the strands, depending on their prior skills and current interests. Others will wish to work on all the strands at once.

Some readers will be working with a mentor, perhaps their subject leader, or head of department or faculty, perhaps a specialist professional tutor, with this book being a workbook supporting both parties. Others may be working on their own, perhaps even as the only specialist history teacher in the school, and the book will be very much a self-help book.

The Oxford University School of Education was instrumental in introducing the idea of mentoring as a way of supporting initial and in-service training. See Brown (1995) for further details about this, and Fish (1995) for more on the development of training and more general mentoring issues. Hake, in Dickinson (1992), gives a good brief philosophical overview of the scheme, and she is well aware of historical issues.

Bearing in mind all these different possible uses of the book, the advice is that it be used in the following way:

The sequencing of sections is intended to reflect the most common needs of history teachers during their first years in teaching. Chapters 1 to 3 concentrate on those issues often addressed early on; Chapters 4 to 6 look at issues likely to become more important during the first year, and Chapters 7 and 8 are aimed at the more established 'new' teacher. The assumed skills and experiences, for each Chapter, are tied in to the sequenced expectation, but all the activities can easily be adapted to suit later stages of the PGCE year, or the RQT years.

Activities are intended to support any reader, but should prove particularly useful for teachers working with colleagues – either in a department, or colleagues in other departments, or historians in other schools.

Further guidance is given in Tolley et al (1996f) Chapter 6.

Notes made while working with this book should be kept and used, if possible, as part of a **professional development portfolio**. This will help support appraisal, the targeting of in-service training, applying for promotion, and the whole process of continuing professional development, including seeking accreditation from an HE institution for work-based learning.

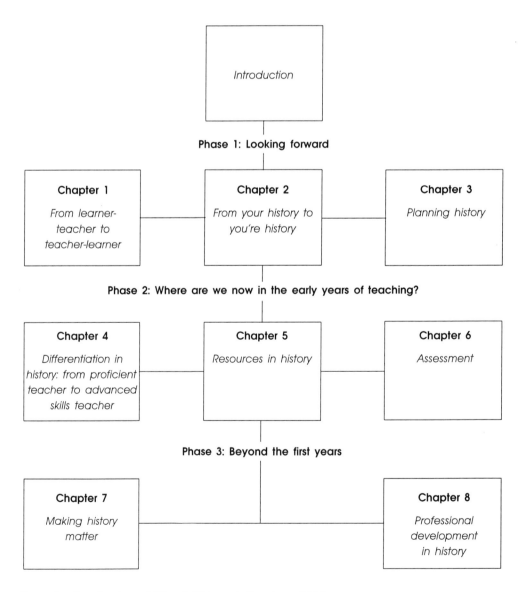

Figure 1 The structure of *Developing as a Teacher of History*

1

From learner-teacher to teacher-learner

Aims

The aims of this Chapter are to:

- clarify the meaning and significance of initial teacher education, and what beginning teachers have got from it;

- embed appropriate attitudes to membership of the teaching profession and professional development within it;

- promote a model of schools as 'learning organisations', recognising the central rôle of research within professional development.

Evidence of standards and competences in training courses and in school

Words like 'competence', 'standard' and 'training', used so much with people doing PGCE and in their NQT year, are not neutral. Some readers may look at the subtitle of this section and make a judgement about the contents on the basis of the use of those three words. **Competence** seems to some a rather low-level and over-technical term; **standard** seems, well, standardised; **training** seems more limited and limiting than **education**. However, as they are used so much, it seems valuable to make the most of them, and if they get stretched a little beyond their limited origins, then that is no bad thing.

Since 1992, the Government has been very clear about the competences with which it expects new teachers to be equipped. There has been a great deal of controversy over the detail of the competences, and over the approach to training and to teaching implied by arranging courses and assessment to fit with these competences. Whatever your individual view of them, however, it is the competences described in 1992 that have dominated training in recent years.

Tolley et al (1996a, p 2) mentions this debate over 'training' or 'education', for people just considering entering training.

During 1997 the Government produced proposals for a new set of *'standards'* statements. However different they are to their predecessors, the new statements do fit the pattern of defining assessment criteria and expecting initial and in-service training to support the collection of evidence for the meeting of those criteria. In working with teachers and trainees, trainers have often said that they enjoyed using the competence statements for particular purposes, even when they were uncertain of the statements' comprehensive validity. One of the most useful activities, described here, is to look for evidence. Whenever teachers assess pupils, or detectives investigate crimes, or archaeologists explore sites, they look for evidence to build up a picture of what happened, and to rule out other events or explanations.

Trainee teachers often have low self esteem. They are liable to a great deal of stress at a time when they are likely to have little money or security. One way to reduce stress is to be very clear about what has been achieved, rather than always thinking about what else needs to be done. That is why building up a portfolio of evidence of standards/competences can be so helpful to trainees. The same, of course, is true of teachers early in their careers, and indeed those later in their careers who also need support. Appraisal, the system common to most schools in which teachers are 'assessed' (the word is avoided in many documents), often takes the form of listing achievements since the last appraisal meeting, and setting targets for the next one. The following activity, then, can be adapted to any stage of your career, but is structured here to suit the period from the end of initial training to the start of the first job.

Burns, in his book on self concept development (Burns, 1982), describes the common dip in self esteem experienced by trainee teachers, as they settle in to teaching practice. He also addresses the vital relationships between the self esteem of pupils and teachers, and how these can change.

Activity

1. Look at the list of the 1997 teaching standards for gaining qualified teacher status, in **Figure 1.1**.

2. Pick out a selection of the standards statements, and write down what evidence you built up, during training, for 'satisfying' that standard. The evidence may have been in your lesson plans, or your evaluations, or the feedback notes given to you by observers, or mark books, or comments made by pupils or colleagues. Most of the evidence should be closely related to the work of pupils. It is worth stressing that 'competent' teaching is properly measured by its effects on pupils' learning. Where the evidence was spoken

See also Tolley et al (1996b pages 47–51;1996d p 5ff), on current strengths and current professional development needs (as a teacher); and Tolley et al (1996f pages 7–9) with stages.

comments, you will appreciate the value of having written them down at the time, in some kind of diary of your experiences. Treat this as a piece of detective work: sometimes it is very much like this, especially if your progress through the course was argued-over, and you or your tutors had to search out particular bits of evidence of individual competences or standards.

Only three or four of the standards should be worked on at a time, as recommended in Tolley et al (1996e p 29) so that each is treated seriously and with sufficient depth. One of the problems with such lists, containing many parts, is that a single piece of evidence might be stretched to cover a multitude of items on the list. This happened with the first versions of the History National Curriculum Attainment Targets, just as it happened with the first versions of the lists of teaching competences. In both cases, the lists were later reduced to a smaller number of (often) more complex individual items.

3. Do the same exercise for your first job, concentrating on the first term or year. Although teachers in their first jobs often say they do more work than they did in training, this work may be narrower: it may not cover the same range of activities as was covered in training. And evidence may be harder to come by, if the school is less particular, for example, about keeping records of lesson plans or whatever.

It is assumed that initial training will have 'exit requirements' for NQT status, ensured by 'base-line assessment', recorded in 'career entry profiles'. These profiles will be the start of 'professional development portfolios', to be carried through a career. These systems are certainly no more bureaucratic than assessment and record-keeping systems for pupils.

4. Compare your two lists. Note that these should be lists of evidence, not just lists of standards. As a history teacher, of course, you can be expected to understand the difficulties of dealing with evidence. You may realise that some of the most important pieces of evidence were never recorded – like that Year 9 pupil who told you your lessons were 'wicked' – or that evidence was hidden or distorted by the requirements of training or the school. Nevertheless, a record of evidence of standards/competences will take you a long way in teaching, especially if it is treated as the basis for reflection, described in the next section.

Such a comparison can easily be converted into a target-setting exercise. This is done below, in the following Activity.

Evidence of reflective practice: your attitude to professional development

Schön (1983) is the key source on the theory of reflective practitioners. His theories related to all professions, especially the medical profession, but have been widely applied to teaching. See for example Fish (1995) and Jones (1994).

Being a reflective practitioner can mean many things, but one way of interpreting it is to look at your attitude to the development of **competences** (used in teacher training from 1992) or of **standards** (used from 1997 or 1998). This may not be the most 'profound' of ways in which to look at reflection, but it certainly has the advantage of making excellent use of the competence/standards statements that could otherwise be treated rather disdainfully by teachers. To be reflective includes looking at your own development as a creative process, trying to improve whilst appreciating what you have already done.

This process will have started with the job. Tolley et al (1996e, pages 9–10) looks at the first days of the job from this perspective.

Activity

1. Look at the standards in **Figure 1.1**. Now, investigate what position you have regarding each one, by completing the table below, **Figure 1.2**. (It is important to do the 'evidence' exercise first, otherwise this exercise might weaken your confidence, by highlighting some of the things still to be done.)

The approach here is complemented by that of Brown and Race (1995), whose book is full of self-assessment exercises, useful at any stage of a career.

2. The logical extension of this task is to commit yourself to gaining evidence of higher standards in the future. Target-setting, a recently fashionable catch-all approach to raising pupil and teacher achievement, is no more than being clear about how things may be expected to change, and how changes can be evaluated. Historians should feel at home with the second of these processes, even if they are a little suspicious of the first of them. Overall, targets can be said to be expressions of hope: as hopes, they are meaningful to the most cynical of teachers, as no-one will readily admit to being hopeless.

When setting targets, it is useful that they are '**SMART**' targets. The acronym SMART is variously defined, but Tolley et al (1996e p 29-quoting Nottinghamshire CC, 1994), say this: **S** is for specific; **M** for manageable and measurable; **A** for appropriate, agreed and achievable; **R** for realistic, relevant and recorded; **T** for time limited. (Action planning is also covered in Tolley et al (1996d pages 8–9), with boxes for professional development need, action to be taken, facilitator, time scale; also objectives, action/review, time scale, personnel, resources.)

Part of the evidence of reflective practice is how you are able to work with colleagues. Most NQTs will be assigned a **mentor**. All will have a manager (usually the subject leader or head of department) responsible in different ways for your progress. They may see their rôles in many ways, as your sympathetic experienced friend, someone who checks on your progress, someone who tells you what to do, someone who can step in in an emergency like the fire brigade, and so on. Such varied rôles will in part be influenced by what you expect or ask of them. A reflective beginning teacher will seek help in developing, rather than simply in avoiding disasters or following orders. Curiosity, and an interest in the views and practices of your mentor, can help both you and the mentor to develop professionally.

Chris Watkins, who has written extensively about mentoring (eg Watkins & Whalley, 1993), has pointed out that the fire brigade nowadays is no longer simply an emergency service, but spends a great deal of time working on fire prevention. It is to be hoped that emergency-oriented mentors will develop in the same way.

An enjoyable debate in the THES of April 1997 has referred to 'virtual' or 'alternative' history, and its relationship to 'conventional' history and to science fiction. See also Ferguson (1997). Perfetti et al (1995) also includes work on reasoning about hypothetical scenarios.

TTA (1997) Standards for the Award of Qualified Teacher Status
June 1997 Version from Annex A to DfEE Circular Letter 1/97

Extracts below are for secondary teachers:

	(A) Subject Knowledge and Understanding	
	For all courses those to be awarded Qualified Teacher Status must, when assessed, demonstrate that they:	
i	have a secure knowledge and understanding of the concepts and skills in their specialist subject(s), at a standard equivalent to degree level to enable them to teach it (them) confidently and accurately at KS3 for trainees on 7–14 courses; KS3 and KS4 and, where relevant, post-16 for trainees on 11–16 or 18 courses; and KS4 and post-16 for trainees on 14–19 courses;	
ii	for English, mathematics or science specialists, have a secure knowledge and understanding of the subject content specified in the relevant Initial Teacher Education National Curriculum;	
iii	have, for their specialist subject(s), a detailed knowledge and understanding of the National Curriculum programmes of study, level descriptions or end of key stage descriptions for KS3 and, where applicable, National Curriculum programmes of study for KS4;	
iv	for RE specialists, have a detailed knowledge of the Model Syllabuses for RE;	
v	are familiar, for their specialist subject(s), with the relevant KS4 and post-16 examination syllabuses and courses, including vocational courses;	
vi	understand, for their specialist subject(s), the framework of 14–19 qualifications and the routes of progression through it;	
vii	understand, for their specialist subject(s), progression from the KS2 programmes of study;	
viii	know and can teach the key skills required for current qualifications, relevant to their specialist subject, for pupils aged 14–19, and understand the contribution that their specialist subject(s) makes to the development of the key skills;	
ix	cope securely with subject-related questions which pupils raise;	
x	are aware of, and know how to access, recent inspection evidence and classroom-relevant research evidence on teaching secondary pupils in their specialist subject(s), and know how to use this to inform and improve their teaching;	
xi	know, for their specialist subject(s), pupils' most common misconceptions and mistakes;	
xii	understand how pupils' learning in the subject is affected by their physical, intellectual, emotional and social development;	
xiii	have, for their specialist subject(s), a secure knowledge and understanding of the content specified in the ITT National Curriculum for Information and Communications Technology in subject teaching;	
xiv	are familiar with subject-specific health and safety requirements, where relevant, and plan lessons to avoid potential hazards.	

Figure 1.1 TTA Standards

(B) Planning, Teaching and Class Management	
Planning	
For all courses those to be awarded Qualified Teacher Status must, when assessed, demonstrate that they:	
a plan their teaching to achieve progression in pupils' learning through: i identifying clear teaching objectives and content, appropriate to the subject matter and the pupils being taught, and specifying how they will be taught and assessed;	
ii setting tasks for whole class, individual and group work, including homework, which challenge pupils and ensure high levels of pupil interest;	
iii setting appropriate and demanding expectations for pupils' learning, motivation and presentation of work;	
iv setting clear targets for pupils' learning, building on prior attainment, and ensuring that pupils are aware of the substance and purpose of what they are asked to do;	

v identifying pupils who:
      • have special educational needs, including specific learning difficulties;
      • are very able;
      • are not fluent in English;
    and knowing where to get help in order to give positive and targeted support;	

b provide clear structures for lessons, and for sequences of lessons, in the short, medium and longer term, which maintain pace, motivation and challenge for pupils;	
c make effective use of assessment information on pupils' attainment and progress in their teaching and in planning future lessons and sequences of lessons;	
d plan opportunities to contribute to pupils' spiritual, moral, personal, social and cultural development;	
e where applicable, ensure coverage of the relevant examination syllabuses and National Curriculum programmes of study.	

Figure 1.1 TTA Standards

(B) Planning, Teaching and Class Management

Teaching and Class Management

For all courses those to be awarded Qualified Teacher Status must, when assessed, demonstrate that they:

f ensure effective teaching of whole classes, and of groups and individuals within the whole class setting, so that teaching objectives are met, and best use is made of available teaching time;	
g monitor and intervene when teaching, to ensure sound learning and discipline;	
h establish and maintain a purposeful working atmosphere;	
i set high expectations for pupils' behaviour, establishing and maintaining a good standard of discipline through well focused teaching and through positive and productive relationships;	
j establish a safe environment which supports learning and in which pupils feel secure and confident;	
k use teaching methods which sustain the momentum of pupils' work and keep all pupils engaged through:	
i stimulating intellectual curiosity, communicating enthusiasm for the subject being taught, fostering pupils' enthusiasm and maintaining pupils' motivation;	
ii matching the approaches used to the subject matter and the pupils being taught;	
iii structuring information well, including outlining content and aims, signalling transitions and summarising key points as the lesson progresses;	
iv clear presentation of content around a set of key ideas, using appropriate subject-specific vocabulary and well chosen illustrations and examples;	
v clear instruction and demonstration, and accurate well-paced explanation;	
vi effective questioning which matches the pace and direction of the lesson and ensures that pupils take part;	
vii careful attention to pupils' errors and misconceptions, and helping to remedy them;	
viii listening carefully to pupils, analysing their responses and responding constructively in order to take pupils' learning forward;	
ix selecting and making good use of textbooks, ICT and other learning resources which enable teaching objectives to be met;	
x providing opportunities for pupils to consolidate their knowledge and maximising opportunities, both in the classroom and through setting well-focused homework, to reinforce and develop what has been learnt;	

… continued

(B) Planning, Teaching and Class Management	
Teaching and Class Management *(continued)*	
xi exploiting opportunities to improve pupils' basic skills in literacy, numeracy and ICT, and the individual and collaborative study skills needed for effective learning, including information retrieval from libraries, texts and other sources;	
xii exploiting opportunities to contribute to the quality of pupils' wider educational development, including their personal, spiritual, moral, social and cultural development;	
xiii setting high expectations for all pupils notwithstanding individual differences, including gender, and cultural and linguistic backgrounds;	
xiv providing opportunities to develop pupils' wider understanding by relating their learning to real and work-related examples;	
l are familiar with the Code of Practice on the identification and assessment of special educational needs and, as part of their responsibilities under the Code, implement and keep records on individual education plans (IEPs) for pupils at stage 2 of the Code and above;	
m ensure that pupils acquire and consolidate knowledge, skills and understanding in the subject;	
n evaluate their own teaching critically and use this to improve their effectiveness.	

Figure 1.1 TTA Standards

(C) Monitoring, Assessment, Recording, Reporting and Accountability	
For all courses those to be awarded Qualified Teacher Status must, when assessed, demonstrate that they:	
a assess how well learning objectives have been achieved and use this assessment to improve specific aspects of teaching;	
b mark and monitor pupils' assigned classwork and homework, providing constructive oral and written feedback, and setting targets for pupils' progress;	
c assess and record each pupil's progress systematically, including through focused observation, questioning, testing and marking, and use records to: i check that pupils have understood and completed the work set;	
ii monitor strengths and weaknesses and use the information gained as a basis for purposeful intervention in pupils' learning;	
iii inform planning;	
iv check that pupils continue to make demonstrable progress in their acquisition of the knowledge, skills and understanding of the subject;	
d are familiar with the statutory assessment and reporting requirements and know how to prepare and present informative reports to parents;	
e where applicable, understand the expected demands of pupils in relation to each relevant level description or end of key stage description, and, in addition, for those on 11–16 or 18 and 14–19 courses, the demands of the syllabuses and course requirements for GCSE, other KS4 courses, and, where applicable, post-16 courses;	
f where applicable, understand and know how to implement the assessment requirements of current qualifications for pupils aged 14–19;	
g recognise the level at which a pupil is achieving, and assess pupils consistently against attainment targets, where applicable, if necessary with guidance from an experienced teacher;	
h understand and know how national, local, comparative and school data, including National Curriculum test data, where applicable, can be used to set clear targets for pupils' achievement;	
i use different kinds of assessment appropriately for different purposes, including National Curriculum and other standardised tests, and baseline assessment where relevant.	

Figure 1.1   TTA Standards

(D) Other Professional Requirements

For all courses those to be awarded Qualified Teacher Status should (note the 'should' rather than 'must' used for categories A, B and C), when assessed, demonstrate that they:

a	have a working knowledge and understanding of:	
	i teachers' professional duties as set out in the current School Teachers' Pay and Conditions document, issued under the School Teachers' Pay and Conditions Act 1991;	
	ii teachers' legal liabilities and responsibilities relating to:	
	• the Race Relations Act 1976;	
	• the Sex Discrimination Act 1975;	
	• Section 7 and Section 8 of the Health and Safety at Work etc Act 1974;	
	• teachers' common law duty to ensure that pupils are healthy and safe on school premises and when leading activities off the school site, such as educational visits, school outings or field trips;	
	• what is reasonable for the purposes of safeguarding or promoting children's welfare (Section 3(5) of the Children Act 1989);	
	• the role of the education service in protecting children from abuse (currently set out in DfEE Circular 10/95 and the Home Office, Department of Health, DfEE and Welsh Office Guidance "Working Together: A guide to arrangements for inter-agency co-operation for the protection of children from abuse 1991");	
	• appropriate physical contact with pupils (currently set out in DfEE Circular 10/95);	
	• appropriate physical restraint of pupils (Section 4 of the Education Act 1997 and DfEE Circular 9/94);	
	• detention of pupils on disciplinary grounds (Section 5 of the Education Act 1997).	
b	have established, during work in schools, effective working relationships with professional colleagues including, where applicable, associate staff;	
c	set a good example to the pupils they teach, through their presentation and their personal and professional conduct;	
d	are committed to ensuring that every pupil is given the opportunity to achieve their potential and meet the high expectations set for them;	
e	understand the need to take responsibility for their own professional development and to keep up to date with research and developments in pedagogy and in the subjects they teach;	

... continued

(D) Other Professional Requirements *(continued)*	
f understand their professional responsibilities in relation to school policies and practices, including those concerned with pastoral and personal safety matters, including bullying;	
g recognise that learning takes place inside and outside the school context, and understand the need to liaise effectively with parents and other carers and with agencies with esponsibility for pupils' education and welfare;	
h are aware of the role and purpose of school governing bodies.	

Figure 1.1 TTA Standards

Attitudes to Standards

(A) Subject Knowledge and Understanding

Standard (see Figure 1.1)	I've demonstrated this for a long time	I've recently 'cracked' this	I think I'm just about getting the hang of this	I intend working on this	I give this the lowest priority at this stage
i					
ii					
iii					
iv					
v					
vi					
vii					
viii					
ix					
x					
xi					
xii					
xiii					
xiv					

Figure 1.2 Attitudes to TTA Standards

Attitudes to Standards

(B) Planning, Teaching and Class Management Planning

Standard (see Figure 1.1)	I've demonstrated this for a long time	I've recently 'cracked' this	I think I'm just about getting the hang of this	I intend working on this	I give this the lowest priority at this stage
a					
i					
ii					
iii					
iv					
v ● SEN					
● very able					
● not fluent in English					
● how help					
b					
c					
d					
e					

Figure 1.2 Attitudes to TTA Standards

Attitudes to Standards

**(B) Planning, Teaching and Class Management
Teaching and Class Management**

Standard (see Figure 1.1)	I've demonstrated this for a long time	I've recently 'cracked' this	I think I'm just about getting the hang of this	I intend working on this	I give this the lowest priority at this stage
f					
g					
h					
i					
j					
k i					
ii					
iii					
iv					
v					
vi					
vii					
viii					
ix					
x					
xi					
xii					
xiii					
xiv					
l					
m					
n					

Figure 1.2 Attitudes to TTA Standards

Attitudes to Standards

(C) Monitoring, Assessment, Recording, Reporting and Accountability

Standard (see Figure 1.1)	I've demonstrated this for a long time	I've recently 'cracked' this	I think I'm just about getting the hang of this	I intend working on this	I give this the lowest priority at this stage
a					
b					
c i					
ii					
iii					
iv					
d					
e					
f					
g					
h					
i					

Figure 1.2 Attitudes to TTA Standards

Attitudes to Standards

(D) Other Professional Requirements

Standard (see Figure 1.1)	I've demonstrated this for a long time	I've recently 'cracked' this	I think I'm just about getting the hang of this	I intend working on this	I give this the lowest priority at this stage
a i					
ii • RRA					
• SDA					
• health & safety at work					
• on & off site					
• welfare					
• protect from abuse					
• contact					
• restraint					
• detention					
b					
c					
d					
e					
f					
g					
h					

Figure 1.2 Attitudes to TTA Standards

Macdonald et al (1989) is my
favourite example of purposeful,
indeed passionate, educational
research that is yet systematic and
well grounded. The research was
commissioned after a murder, and
ties this in to every aspect of
education.

Attributed to Robert Dubin, but the
exact reference seems lost.

Your place in the learning organisation: life is an action research project

There is a significant body of literature on industrial and commercial management that refers to the need to be a **learning organisation**. Connoisseurs of irony will not be surprised to learn the theory of the learning organisation was not initially applied to schools. Yet schools are full of learning teachers, and are fed by and feed themselves on research all the time. This may be called 'appraisal', 'policy documents', 'school development plans', 'responses to new initiatives', 'National Curriculum documents', 'conference/INSET reports', 'lesson planning', or much else. In any case, we expect children to learn; adults should expect to learn too. In Senge (1990) a learning organisation is described as incorporating personal mastery, mental models, a shared vision, team learning, and systems thinking (the *'fifth discipline'* that gives the book its title).

Think about those teachers and others working in education whom you know were not prepared to learn, and those schools not prepared to develop (or not prepared to develop as a result of thinking). Use this thought to help you to see the necessity of research.

Learning is not a uniform process, and being a **learning teacher** involves the quality of understanding where you are on the **learning curve** for each aspect of your work. The four learning curve positions, described in Tolley et al (1996b, p 6) are:

- **unconscious incompetence** *(I don't know I can't);*
- **conscious incompetence** *(I know I can't);*
- **conscious competence** *(I know I can);*
- **unconscious competence** *(I can without thinking).*

It is a pleasant game, if feeling insecure amongst colleagues because you are at the second stage, to think that, impressive as they are, your colleagues are just as likely to be at the first stage, behind you, than the third or fourth stage, ahead.

Department of Education and
Science (1989) (the 'Elton Report')
is a superbly written, clear, non-
technical, concise Government
report. A model for any research
and development project, it
combines clear analysis of current
beliefs (of teachers, pupils, parents,
unions, etc) with a sensitive guide
to good practice.

Bell (1987) is a good
comprehensive guide to education
research techniques; Strauss and
Corbin (1990) is helpful on
qualitative research.

Research is normal, and should be 'recognisable'. Research separated from institutions is the equivalent of science fiction: terribly interesting to insiders, but an object of fun for outsiders. What is recommended here is **recognisable research**, therefore, and when the product can be used, it might be called **action research** (ie research deriving from and in turn influencing professional activity). If it is not only useable but used, then it might be called **research and development** work.

Activity

1. Plan a piece of research, of about 2000 words, that fits in with your progress through the NQT year. (See below, Chapter 6, on following this up, as a historian, and further below, Chapter 8, on using this as a springboard for future professional development.) This piece of research will be able to be included in a professional development portfolio, for which formal credit may be given, and it could lead to or form part of other courses or systems of accreditation. The work could valuably be done precisely on your first school, as many PGCE courses require of your first practice school. Such research may include putting the school in the context of current national issues (using, for example, *Times Educational Supplement*), local issues (eg local facilities, faith communities, political groups, etc, using local newspapers and institutions), and intra school issues (eg ethos indicators, approaches to special needs or staff development, etc).

2. Discuss this research with your mentor, subject leader or head of department, being sensitive to their perceived rôle as supporter, checker, teller, etc.

Here, a formal piece of research is recommended, to focus work on continuing professional development. An equally valid, complementary, approach is to maintain a professional journal, a combination of a personal diary and a log of experiences, as described in Tolley et al (1996b) and elsewhere in the series. Formal induction procedures may provide a third approach, and these are outlined, for consideration, in DfEE (1998c).

2

From your history to you're history

Aims

The aims of this Chapter are to:

- *investigate the significance of school history;*

- *help beginning teachers understand the rôle of history across the curriculum;*

- *investigate beginning teachers' own positions with respect to history education.*

> *"I sit with my back to the future, watching*
> *time pouring away into the past. I sit, being helplessly*
> *lugged backwards*
> *through the Debatable Lands of history"*
>
> Norman MacCaig, Crossing the Border

Justifying history

A popular interview question is "Why do you want this job?" a tempting answer is "You need a teacher and I need the money". Almost as popular is the question "How can you justify having history on the curriculum?" It is almost as tempting to give the trivial answer "The Government says we have to teach history at Key Stage 3 and offer it at Key Stage 4". However, this is not sufficient to carry you through the first year of teaching. Apart from anything else, when pupils, or parents, ask you the same question, they are unlikely to be fobbed-off with trivial answers.

So what is history for? National Curriculum documentation justifies every subject in terms of providing a broad and balanced curriculum, promoting spiritual, moral, cultural, mental and physical development of pupils, and preparing them for the opportunities, responsibilities and experiences of adult life. The specific aims of history are stated in various forms, including descriptions of what pupils should be enabled to do within key stages. However, National Curriculum history aims will not satisfy teachers looking for a detailed subject philosophy.

This book is not aiming to promote a single view of the rôle of history in school, but to help beginning teachers appreciate the issues in the context of their first jobs. It is always worth asking yourself how your work helps fulfil these basic aims. Questions based on them are of course also popular with OfSTED inspectors. Try not to be seduced into thinking that history should be taught 'for its own sake', unless you are clear about what the 'it' is.

Lee et al (1992) covers a fine debate on the aims and rôles of history. Any NQT who did not read the book in training could valuably read it in the first year of teaching. The complexity of some parts of the book should not put readers off, and the first and last Chapters put the whole debate in context with great clarity. Haydn et al (1997) Chapter 2 is similarly useful.

Dean (1995) Chapter 1 has a particularly clear account, easily appreciated by non-specialists. Chapter 2 covers the National Curriculum, too.

See also the work in Chapter 5 on primary liaison.

Activity

1. Complete the table in **Figure 2.1**, on the purpose of history teaching. In your own words, describe the justifications for teaching history.

2. Complete the second table in **Figure 2.2**, on evidence for meeting individual National Curriculum key stage descriptors. The work on Key Stages 1 and 2 is intended to help beginning teachers build on pupils' previous work. It can only be done with the cooperation of staff in primary schools, and building up these links is itself valuable.

The purpose of history teaching	
The purpose of history teaching as described in the National Curriculum.	
The purpose of history teaching as described in the GCSE syllabus used.	
The purpose of history teaching as described in the departmental handbook.	
The purpose of history teaching stated in or implied by the main textbook series used in Key Stage 3.	
The purpose of history teaching stated in or implied by the main textbook series used in Key Stage 4.	
My own beliefs about the purpose of history teaching, within *this* school.* (Take account of NC and departmental/school policies. If the activity is easy, it is not worth doing: justifying history should be complex).	
My own beliefs about the purpose of history teaching, in an *ideal* context. (Your views on intrinsic/extrinsic aims, on preparing pupils for an open society, on doubt, on a love of the past, etc, can have full rein).	

*   The gap between the 'real' and 'ideal', to be worked on in this exercise, and suggested elsewhere in this Chapter and beyond, is derived from theories of learning. For example Vygotsky (whose work is well described in Daniels, 1996) writes of a 'zone of proximal development' (ZPD). The ZPD is a way of describing learning as a movement from dependent to independent understanding – ie from needing help to understand (or do, or describe, etc) to needing no such help. Where a teacher sees the purpose of teaching history as entirely 'given' by a school exam board, the understanding could be said to be 'dependent'. Learning, as an NQT, can therefore involve developing a more 'independent' understanding of history teaching. In the activity, above, this involves describing externally imposed views on the purpose of history teaching; then your *own* version of these views; then a version of your views that should stand *independent* of the immediate context of the school. In a similar way, Fisher (1998) in the companion volume for geography teachers in this series talks about autonomy as a key dimension of professional development..

Figure 2.1 The purpose of history teaching

Evidence for meeting National Curriculum key stage descriptors

This is a history of history, and should be done in conjunction with primary schools. Record evidence you have found, in your own school and in feeder schools, of pupils having been given opportunities to develop as learners of history. Many feeders produce pupils with distinct approaches and attitudes to history – and studying them can make secondary teachers more aware of their own approaches. Understanding progression from KS2 to KS3 is also a requirement set out in the Standards for QTS.

Key stage descriptors	Evidence
Key Stage 1: Pupils should be given opportunities to develop an awareness of the past and of the ways in which it was different from the present. They should be helped to set their study of the past in a chronological framework and to understand some of the ways in which we find out about the past.	
Key Stage 2: Pupils should be taught about important episodes and developments in Britain's past, from Roman to modern times, about ancient civilisations and the history of other parts of the world. They should be helped to develop a chronological framework by making links across the different study units. They should have opportunities to investigate local history and to learn about the past from a range of sources of information.	
Key Stage 3: Pupils should be taught about changes in the economy, society, culture and political structure of Britain from the early Middle Ages to the twentieth century. They should be taught about aspects of European and non-European history, and to make links and connections between historical events and changes in the different periods and areas studied. They should be given opportunities to use their historical knowledge to evaluate and use sources of information, and to construct narratives, descriptions and explanations of historical events and developments.	

Figure 2.2 Evidence for key stage descriptors

History in the whole curriculum: humanities and beyond

History teachers should be aware of their positions in schools. In a school hierarchy, the positions from NQT to head of department (HoD) or subject leader are generally expected to be sectional, with these staff trying to promote the special interests of their subject or department. Senior managers are usually defined as the Head, deputy heads and senior teachers, although schools have many ways of defining their hierarchies. The senior management team (or SMT) may be expected to take a whole-school perspective on issues, and to act as arbiter between sectional interests.

As a beginning teacher, as indeed any position below SMT level, it is worth trying to exploit both sectional and whole-school perspectives. The subject does indeed have a special position in the curriculum, and an NQT can often highlight this position – as more experienced teachers may have lost some of their subject-based 'inspiration'. However, when it comes to inter-departmental and whole-school issues, the NQT is likely to be in an even better position. Any induction system will most likely include those issues of great importance across the school, such as behaviour policies, equal opportunities, language across the curriculum, developing independent learning, or whatever. As a history teacher, you can build on such induction to make the subject more inclusive, fed by and feeding other subjects.

Activity

1. Focus on one, or perhaps two, aspects of history that make the subject (and the department) special or potentially special in the school. Put together a 'bid' to promote this aspect. It may be a bid for money to set up a resources-base, or for ICT facilities to support a local history project, or for time for pupils to put together an assembly on a historical theme.

    The reason for describing this as a bid is to help you to fit in with the most common style of developing work in schools. Schools are expected to have development plans, usually covering two or three years, produced in the 'boxes' style familiar to readers of curriculum plans. A teacher who can write a bid in that style will not only prove useful for their HoD, but will be likely to find it easier to fit in with all levels of the school's hierarchy. (See for example Hargreaves & Hopkins (1991) on school development work.)

2. Focus on one cross-curricular theme to which you and history can contribute particularly effectively. Put together a bid, as above, promoting this. You may wish to work in partnership with colleagues in other departments, including NQTs and RQTs with whom you are working on the induction programme. It may be a bid for a 'cross curricular' day – perhaps a citizenship day, or an equal opportunities day – or it may be work on developing good practice in setting homework, or differentiation in teaching. (See also the work in Chapter 7, below.)

See Copeland (1993) on geography, Pownall and Hutson (1992) on science, and Copeland (1991) on maths. Each of these booklets, produced by English Heritage, justifies cross-curricular work at historic sites. They provide, inter alia, wonderful arguments for inter-departmental trips and visits, sharing work and costs. This is particularly useful for small secondary and all primary schools.

Start talking to someone about history. How often will they say "Ah, I had a history teacher once who ...". The way in which the teacher and the subject are bound together is highlighted by the surprise shown by pupils when a history teacher is also discovered to have another talent (such as music or sport), or is even found to have a life outside school and, my goodness, goes shopping.

Doing, being, and learning about history: does it make a difference how much I know?

When studying history in higher education, there is a tendency to see yourself as the 'subject' and history as the 'object'. You are 'doing' history. Early in your experience of teaching, you may have shifted your perspective, seeing yourself still as the subject, but the pupils as the object, and history as the 'verb' – ie what you do with the pupils. Later on, the history may come to have a smaller place in your concerns. Some teachers see history as almost incidental, with the generic teaching skills or the personal and general academic progress of the pupils being more important than the topics taught. However, if the pupils are to learn history in your classes, they (and you) must still see history as important. For the rest of their lives, many of your pupils will associate history with you. So, to go back to the grammatical metaphor, far from you being the 'subject' with history the 'object', once you get into teaching, you become the pupils' 'object', identified wholly with history.

In this sense, the sense in which you are history, your attitude to developing subject knowledge need not simply be about 'learning a great deal of history', but rather should be about getting inside the subject in such a way as to help the pupils get inside with you.

Activity

1. Convince yourself that you are still a historian. You may be doing continuing research for a degree, or other work as a professional historian, but few teachers manage this. Being a historian may mean reading-up for topics to be taught (and this is always a good learning exercise), finding out about the history of the school or its area or where you live. It may mean, sadly, that holidays become research opportunities. (It is difficult for history teachers to go on holiday to Venice, for example, without planning lessons on East-West trade routes.) Write in a professional journal, if one is kept, or as a separate exercise, about how you are a historian.

2. Devise an exercise to convince your pupils that you are history. You may be happy to rôle-play historical figures: a useful task is to get pupils to devise interview questions, which you, in rôle, will answer. (John Fines has talked about the joys of playing Queen Victoria, for primary pupils.) You may, more directly, be interviewed as yourself, being asked, for example, about how society has changed in the last ten (or 20, or 30) years. Creating a photographic *History of the 20th Century*, using your own family photos, is surprisingly easy for most teachers – at least those still on speaking terms with older relatives. Write down how, for your pupils, you are history.

The 'tourist' industry has in many areas become the 'heritage' industry, to exploit such learning opportunities.

See Tolley et al (1996b) and other books in the same series, for full guidance on keeping professional journals. The 'professional development portfolio', starting with a 'career entry profile', has become central to in-service teacher education.

Subject knowledge is one way that people are often judged as subject specialists. Clearly, being a more knowledgeable historian is something of an advantage. However, the 'amount' of history you know, or the breadth or your knowledge, is not as straightforwardly advantageous as people might think. Two stories have been told, in different versions, for many years. The present author has heard both in the last couple of years. Individually, the stories are not surprising; what is interesting is that they can both be told.

It has become fashionable in recent years to talk about the curriculum as either knowledge-based or skills-based. Historians are unlikely to have a 'simple' view of knowledge that would allow such a clear-cut division.

Story A: In answer to the question "Who is your best teacher?", a pupil names Ms X, saying that she is best because she knows everything about the subject, and you can ask her anything and there will be an answer.

Story B: In answer to the question "Who is your best teacher?", a pupil names Ms Y, saying that she is best because she admits that she has difficulty with the subject, and has to work everything out carefully herself. This makes her explain everything very clearly, and makes her very sympathetic to pupils having difficulties understanding a topic.

The moral of the first story seems to be that you should strive to know as much as you can about your subject; the moral of the second story seems to be that lacking knowledge or skill helps make you a better teacher. The moral of the two stories, however, is different: it is that whatever level of knowledge or skill you have in your subject, you can exploit that level and use it to make yourself a better teacher. Hence, it is less a matter of how clever or knowledgeable you are, than how wise you are.

This is not a position held by all writers in the field. Dean (1995) presents strong evidence that levels of subject knowledge and teaching skill are strongly correlated. However, it is difficult, I would suggest, to tease out any causal relationship between the two that avoids the complex effects of self-esteem and professional regard. Perhaps it is true that teachers with less evidence of subject knowledge in history are also likely to have less evidence of teaching skill in history. But this might be the result of their feeling 'low status' history teachers, rather than actually being 'ill-equipped' to be expert teachers.

Activity

1. Fill in the table below in **Figure 2.3**. It is worth doing at any stage of a teaching career, and can certainly be repeated during the early years of your teaching.

Best and worst history topics		
Best topic:		**at (date):**
Advantages of knowing a lot:		Still need to learn:
Worst topic:		**at (date):**
Key points to research:		Advantages of knowing little:

Figure 2.3 Best and worst history topics

3
Planning history

Aims

The aims of this Chapter are to:

- *improve the time and stress management skills of beginning teachers;*
- *promote effective planning in history teaching;*
- *help beginning teachers appreciate the value of curriculum planning in terms of effective teaching/learning and their own time/stress management.*

This Chapter looks at ways in which planning is able to enhance and unify history teaching in a school. Along with Chapters 1 and 2, it is intended for the early terms of teaching. Chapter 4 looks at the diversity of skills and approaches amongst teachers and pupils, and is intended for later use. However, Chapters 3 and 4 are really two perspectives on the same issue: how to improve the quality of teaching and learning, ensuring access to all, whilst recognising the various experiences that the participants will inevitably have.

To plan effectively, it is important to consider these three issues:

- *how does planning help save time and work?*
- *how do your plans fit in with (and enhance) the plans of others?*
- *how will your plans be reviewed and changed?*

Alfred Schutz talks about 'multiple realities' (in eg Schutz, 1973) to describe the diversity of views or positions held by different people in the same position. When planning, always consider how your plans will take account of these different views.

Activity

1. Write down exactly how many minutes or hours you spend on school work, during the seven days immediately preceding or immediately following reading this. (It is better, if you can remember well enough, to look at the preceding week.) The average teacher, according to recent surveys, works for about 52 hours a week during term time. (If you like, discuss with your colleagues a 'sensible' number of hours, given the circumstances of your school, for teachers to work. If you do this, then you can replace '52 hours' with your alternative number in the following activity.)

   Teachers, in common with pupils, seem to be very reluctant to do this activity. Is this because they prefer to think they are overworked, rather than actually measure their work and do something about it?

2. Decide whether you think your work is comparable to that of your colleagues, or if you think it is systematically more effective or less effective. Consider this, alongside the number of hours worked. If the total number of hours worked is higher than the average, and you think your work is particularly effective, then you have a viable explanation. If the hours are high, but the effectiveness is low, then you are probably too stressed to work effectively. If the hours are lower than average, then you may either be particularly good at planning your work, or you may have a ready-made explanation of why your work is less effective than that of your colleagues.

   Comparing oneself with one's colleagues is not intended to undermine the evidence that teaching is more stressful than comparable jobs. A *Sunday Times* survey, researched by Cary L Cooper and published on 18 May 1997, suggested that teaching was the fourth most stressful job (after prison officers, police and social workers) out of 104 occupations studied, and that the job had also had the fourth biggest increase in stress between 1985 and 1997.

'Work smarter, not harder' is a slogan taken up by British Telecom (and referred to in Tolley et al, 1996e p 12) and is a useful catch-all response to apparent over-work. It is not 'how much' that matters, as 'how well' and, however much you work, 'how much before the deadlines'. Spending the same number of hours before the deadline (eg writing reports) as others spend after the deadline, will give you a reputation for working harder than them. (Be warned, however, that BT now uses the terrifying slogan 'wake up to the 24-hour society!')

3. Look at the results of this activity on time management. Consider what proportion of your work is affected by planning or lack of planning. Now consider whether the work so affected could be enhanced by more effective planning by you, better co-ordination of the planning you do with others, or an overhaul of your whole planning and preparation process.

The sections in this Chapter look at chronology, content, the use of evidence, perspectives, and engagement. These are of course not comprehensive, but between them enough planning issues are brought up that could be applied to any other area requiring planning. It is absolutely vital to plan within your department's schemes of work and syllabuses: plan to exploit their potential and enhance them, not replace them.

A complementary exercise is in Tolley et al (1996e pages 8–9).

Activity

1. Get all the curriculum plans for history in Key Stages 3, 4 and 5 (if the school continues beyond 16). Highlight what you already feel is most helpful and supportive in these plans.

2. Now, highlight (in a different colour) those parts that you feel most need developing.

All the work in this Chapter should be done in the context of the activity above, using curriculum plans in positive ways.

Time marches on: planning for chronology

Helping pupils to gain a sense of the passage of time seems like one of the simplest, yet in practice can be one of the hardest, elements of history teaching. Planning for teaching chronology is particularly valuable, as planning itself is a matter of putting things in (date) order, and giving them a sense of structure.

If anyone says how difficult it is teaching about the Ancient Romans to pupils in the 1990s, remind them of how difficult it is teaching them about the years immediately before they were born. It is hardly any harder. As for me, World War Two is getting closer and closer. I was brought up in the 1960s, and at that time, World War Two seemed to me to be ancient history. Now, in the 1990s, my memories of that time make the War seem very close. There were bomb sites around my home town, utility furniture in the house, and an economy based on principles more-or-less agreed at the end of the War. Everyone of my parents' generation had vivid memories (and many stories) of the War, and older people (of my grandparents' generation) were telling stories of World War One and earlier. Yet such recent events were so distant, then.

Approaches to teaching chronology

There are two important aspects of chronology: the sense of events being placed in order, marked by time, and the sense of the passage of time being a dynamic process, a process of change. The first set of activities looks at the placement of events in time.

Activity

It was reported in the TES of 30 May 1997 that there have been protests in Italy against the Government's decrees requiring all secondary schools to teach only post–1918 history. When combined with the Government statements in the UK, suggesting that 'history' stops in the mid–1960s, Anglo-Italian history might end up with the chronologically squashed prospect of less than 50 years of history. An interesting idea.

1. **Do a chronology audit for yourself.** (You may also wish to do it with colleagues, friends or family.) A simple method is to get 25 sheets of paper, and title each one with a century, covering the current century and the previous 24 centuries (and please feel free to go further back). Write down one item on each sheet of paper – it may be an identifiable event, or it may be a period or the time of flourishing of a culture or economic system. If you can write down one item on each sheet, go on to a second item. When you have found yourself stuck, you can specialise, and write down several events for those centuries you know better. When you run out of information from your memory, you may want to have a short dash around your books or other sources of information, to stop yourself being too embarrassed.

   Then, look at this chronology. Write down when you think you first found out about each item listed. You will then have a rough history of your own knowledge of the placement of events in time. This element of the activity is related to 'lifemapping', referred to in Fisher (1998) as deriving from the work of Michael Kompf.

2. **Do a chronology audit with one of your classes.** It is a good idea to do it once from memory, perhaps with groups of pupils thinking about groups of centuries, and again for homework, perhaps with individual pupils finding out about one century each. If this work is done with some style, then the outcome could be used for a display, Bayeux Tapestry style, along a corridor or around a room.

   The class can then have a sense of their collective knowledge of the placement of events in time.

3. **Compare the class chronology with your own.** What sort of differences do you see? Often, pupils will see history in terms of short clearly identifiable events, while adults will have more of a sense of periods and eras. Consider what this tells you about a sense of chronology.

You might also look for differences between different groups of pupils. Useful research could investigate changes in pupils' sense of chronology at different ages. Of course, it would be inappropriate for beginning teachers to expect a conclusion in the form "all children in Year 7 ..." or, even worse, "all children in Year 7 must be able to ...".

Pupils should enjoy finding out that any two historians are likely to give a different list of 'the most important events/dates'. Of many such exercises, the *TES* of 13 April 1990 produced a clear example, asking five historians, at the time of the publication of the history National Curriculum, to list the dates 'to be carved in stone' for pupils.

The passage of time is a dynamic process, however, not simply a collection of isolated moments. How can history teachers help pupils appreciate and understand this sense of **change over time**? Beginning teachers can make use of their own experiences of change, during the first years of teaching, to help with this aspect of teaching. The NQT year is often a year of rapid, sometimes exciting, sometimes painful, change: you are likely to have learned a great deal about other people and procedures, and you are likely to have changed your own views on them. This sense of dynamic change – it is tempting to use the term 'struggle' – is also a characteristic of childhood and adolescence.

Activity

1. Arrange for pupils to describe an important time of change for them. The first day at secondary school is a good example: pupils often remember it vividly, and can describe their expectations and fears and how they dealt with them.

2. Ask the pupils to analyse the changes, looking for relationships of cause and effect, multiple causes, ambiguity of interpretation, perspective, etc. A starting point for the assessment or analysis of change is the exercise in **Figure 3.1**. This is valuable as an exercise for teachers, too.

3. Ask the pupils to compare their results in small groups. Are there patterns emerging – including patterns related to the difficulty of gaining a clear understanding of the processes of change over time?

4. Now ask them, in small groups, to do the same exercise for a key turning point or event in history. They should choose an event with which they are familiar – and they may even want to study an event from the very recent past.

Rush (1994) gives a lively account of a first day at school, though this might need a little editing if it is to be read out in class.

The exercise might be thought to be encouraging a Whig view of history, the view satirised in **1066 And All That**, *looking for 'good' and 'bad' changes. If handled carefully, however, the exercise can provide valuable insight into the nature of change and of the process of interpreting or evaluating changes.*

Periodic tables: planning for content

There is a mass of 'content' that, in the early years of the National Curriculum, often terrified teachers into talking too quickly and never stopping to look at anything in depth. Most teachers now realise the advantages of a mixture of in-depth work and 'broad brush strokes' to cover the whole stipulated period. However, in planning for history, many still try simply to list 'everything that happened', with the proviso that "we won't of course get through it all". Effective planning needs to do more that this. For example, by stipulating group project work on one aspect of a topic, with different small groups of pupils investigating different areas, and with each group reporting back their results to the rest of the class, a teacher can 'plan' for a large amount of subject content in a surprisingly short amount of lesson time.

Outline history, the 'broad brush strokes' approach, need not be superficial. An overview of a long period should be complex and fascinating, just as an overview of the countryside, from an aircraft, can be complex and fascinating. The theories of fractal geometry, popularised in Gleick (1987), can be used to explain how some objects (like clouds or coastlines) are equally complex at different scales. History, done in depth or in outline, may have some similarities, although of course the level of individual human experience and motivation has a special significance. (See Walsh in Lee et al, 1992 p 36, on the love of past people; see Lee et al, 1992 p 4 on the importance of the overview.)

The analysis of change		
	Change for the better – in which ways?	Change for the worse – in which ways?
Change that was just about inevitable – and why		
Change that might not have happened – and why		

Figure 3.1 The analysis of change

Activity

1. Pick the 'fullest' topic you will have to teach, and plan ways in which you have, or you could have, covered the topic using group work as described above.

2. Consider what were (or what will be) the most effective aspects of such work, and what disadvantages it has. For example, some teachers say that the presentations, though valuable for the presenters, may not 'teach' the rest of the class much. Work out ways of overcoming such difficulties.

Digging for victory: planning for using evidence

Most professional historians work with a mass of evidence, yet also talk about the 'nuggets' they find: a small number of pieces of evidence that have transformed their view of a topic. Very experienced history teachers may have a wealth of evidence to hand on every conceivable topic, but as a beginning teacher, you may have less, or more narrowly focused, evidence to work with. Concentrate, therefore, on planning to have a small number of key pieces of evidence, spread across groups and throughout your first years of teaching.

Activity

1. Dig out 38 bits of evidence from your department, home (including books you own, and the cellar, back garden, etc), museums, and so on. These 38 should cover the 38 teaching weeks of the year, and so should be well spread over periods. They may be quotations, pictures, artefacts, videos, or much else. Record them on the table below in **Figure 3.2**.

2. Work out one interesting thing to be learnt from each piece of evidence, and record these uses in the adjoining boxes.

History without evidence is like a music lesson with no music, or food technology with no food. There is now such easy access to evidence, in books and using ICT, that there is no reason to say "I can't find any sources on …" The first year of teaching can therefore be one of practising making the most effective use of evidence, rather than one of searching out materials.

Get it in perspective: planning for dealing with different viewpoints

It is possible that new history teachers are in the best and the worst position to deal with competing historical perspectives. Being new, the teacher is more likely to be prepared to consider a wide variety of styles of teaching and learning, and to welcome debate and disagreement amongst pupils. However, NQTs are also more likely to feel less secure in their schools, and (like all teachers new to a school) less confident in their knowledge of pupils. Admitting to historical uncertainties, meat and drink to professional historians, can be thought weakness in a history teacher working with pupils who are always quick to spot any weakness their teachers display.

Rather than being swallowed up by uncertainty or relativism, plan to cover at least one key dispute for every group you teach. There are popular teaching/learning techniques to complement this work. More or less formal debates may be used, with pupils presenting alternative viewpoints, and these debates can be enhanced if video- or audio-taped. Alternative newspaper front pages (eg an English and French newspaper covering the death of Napoleon) may incidentally teach pupils about the mass media, and should make for a good display, too. Writing imaginative diaries, as if by participants in events who might have different positions, can help with engagement and empathy. Producing a rôle-play, involving some sort of argument or discussion, can get pupils involved who would otherwise have difficulty appreciating 'perspectives' work.

Display is used by many history teachers to make their classrooms into inanimate teachers. See Hodgson (1988) and Tolley et al (1996b p 30) on general display issues. Organisations such as the Imperial War Museum and English Heritage have superb display resources.

Croall (1992) gives a lively account of the self-explanatory 'Dig Where You Stand' scheme. This should encourage teachers to look for evidence close at hand. Hinton (1990) is a fine book on the use of evidence, written for GCSE students.

See also below, Chapter 5 on resources. The intention of the current Chapter is to make a relatively simple collection, and of the later Chapter to consider the collection of resources in much more detail.

See Burns (1982) on self-esteem.

Perfetti et al (1995) includes a Chapter about learning and reasoning about controversy. Carrington and Troyna (1988) covers more general issues of dealing with controversy. The book, usefully, refers to the views of young children (including pre-school children) and thereby explodes the myth of controversy being a predominantly adult interest.

38 pieces of evidence to be used in history lessons

Evidence: / Use:				
1	9	17	25	32
2	10	18	26	33
3	11	19	27	34
4	12	20	28	35
5	13	21	29	36
6	14	22	30	37
7	15	23	31	38
8	16	24		

Figure 3.2   Evidence used in history lessons

Developing as a Teacher of History

Activity

1. Pick out or produce from scratch one piece of 'viewpoints' work for each topic you teach during the year. The same technique (eg a debate) may be used more than once, but do be sure to envisage distinct outcomes.

2. For one of the above pieces of work with a class, work out very carefully in advance how to record and assess the contributions of the pupils. Chapter 6, below, includes far more details on assessment. At this stage, it is most important to realise that work of any kind in history can and should be recordable, and that recording and assessment should cover the whole range of teaching and learning techniques.

Giving it fizz: planning for engagement

> "Boredom is ... a vital problem for the moralist, since half the sins of mankind are caused by the fear of it"
>
> Bertrand Russell, The Conquest of Happiness

However interested you are in a topic, and however interesting you think your teaching should be, the judges of interest are the pupils. "This is boring" can kill a lesson, or even an NQT. Sometimes people judge a teacher by how enthusiastic they are, but enthusiasm that is not transferred simply means being boring. Engaging pupils, or having 'infectious' enthusiasm, need not be a mysterious, magical quality, like charisma. Engagement can and should be planned for, and should be part of just about every lesson. An old-fashioned football manager was reported as having given the same pep-talk to his team at half-time in every match for many years: "Give it fizz, lads, give it fizz" was all he would say. That seems like good advice for teachers, too.

'Death by a thousand worksheets' is the phrase used to describe one method of teaching which is unproblematic when used as one of a number of strategies, but which can be exceptionally boring when it is the only technique used.

Three key techniques for engaging pupils in history are:

*   questioning;

*   giving presentations;

*   making pupils into teachers.

Questions engage people. As a matter of class management, teachers quickly learn that asking pupils questions can get them on task, or at least get them off inappropriate tasks. It was a very experienced and confident teacher who reported that, on being threatened by a knife-wielding pupil, asked him "Is that a new jacket you're wearing?" The pupil, by report, entered into the conversation and forgot about the knife. Historians are likely to view history as an attempt to answer important questions. However, pupils may be presented with history as if all the questions have already been answered, and they are simply there to learn them. Therefore, the following activities focus on using questions to engage pupils.

Activity

1. Pick a set of lessons taught during the previous week, covering different year groups. For each one, write down what the most important question was related to that topic. Again, for each one, can you say, honestly, that the pupils knew what the key question was? How? Was the key question on the board or in the materials or on the display boards?

2. Think about other ways in which your pupils are 'engaged' by the use of questions in your classes.

The SHP textbooks for Key Stage 3 (eg Shephard et al, 1991) helpfully arrange their material into 'big' questions, with the question usually displayed at the top of each page.

Giving presentations. For personal and social reasons, as well as for the development of historical skills, it is worth encouraging pupils to present their work to other pupils. There are many ways of doing this, from presenting work informally to a friend, in pair work, to presenting work to the whole school in an assembly. How have your pupils been allowed/encouraged to present their work to other pupils? As a rule of thumb, no pupil should be able to get through a term's worth of history without doing a presentation. It is helpful to make some such presentations into formal assessment exercises, with the presentations perhaps taped or

Working as teams and presenting to colleagues can both be seen as forms of peer tutoring. (See also Topping, 1988.) Research seems to suggest that such approaches are particularly effective at helping pupils learn.

videoed. It is also useful to make the preparation of presentations a regular homework task, as the forthcoming presentation generally provides sufficient incentive to complete the homework.

An extension of the use of presentations in class is **the use of pupils as teachers**. A mainstay of sarcastic teachers over the years, when a pupil has disrupted a lesson, has been to say "Why don't you come up here and take the lesson yourself?". It would be good to rescue this idea from its use as sarcasm. Pupils make good teachers, and they can teach their peers or younger pupils or family members. You may even be able to get them to teach other teachers. Teaching is always engaging, as teachers of course know.

Activity

1. Look through the schemes of work for the pupils you teach, and work out where pupils are or could be given opportunities to teach something to somebody. As GCSE history often covers periods and topics worked on in Year 9, it is particularly worth considering using GCSE pupils to teach elements of Year 9 schemes of work. As GCSE and A Level history requires such skill in the use of evidence, it is well worth using such pupils to teach evidence skills to Year 7.

Engagement, then, can be planned for, yet it can never be guaranteed. Teachers can be upset to find that pupils, bored with a specially constructed board game related to the Norman invasion, find copying off the board positively thrilling. This is not in general because board games are less engaging than copying; pupils may simply feel insecure with a board game and secure with copying. When planning for engagement, it is therefore important to provide a variety of tasks, and not to rely on artificially 'exciting' tasks.

4

Differentiation in history: from proficient teacher to advanced skills teacher

Aims

The aims of this Chapter are to:

- *help beginning teachers clarify their rôles as teachers responsible for diverse learners;*
- *promote the effective use of the diverse skills and knowledge of teaching colleagues;*
- *enable beginning teachers to promote more independent learning skills of their pupils.*

Pedagogy for a purpose

The last Chapter looked at planning for particular aspects of history, with Chapters 1 to 3 all focusing on supporting the first terms of teaching. Chapters 4 to 6 are aimed, broadly, at later stages. Chapter 4 in particular complements Chapter 1, stressing pedagogy. The purpose of school is learning, not teaching: pedagogy (or 'the science of teaching') helps us focus on techniques for aiding learning, not simply techniques for teaching.

Differentiation simply means taking account of the mixture of abilities in your lesson. Every group of people (however they are selected) is a 'mixed ability' group. This is not a problem. If you see it as a problem, then that is a problem. The teacher is the conductor of an orchestra of different instruments: no-one goes to a concert to see the conductor alone, or to see the orchestra all playing the same tune on one instrument.

Brian Simon, in Moon & Shelton Mayes (1994) writes about the absence in England of a 'science of teaching', and how that works against the possibility of developing the most effective teaching. "Teaching … must always take the child forward" (p 19).

Action point

Extend the musical metaphor further. Think about your view of yourself as a teacher: are you a conductor or a soloist? Some teachers see themselves as conductors. This fits with a popular view of the etymology of 'education', ie 'leading out' pupils, from the Latin *educere*. The word is probably in fact derived from the Latin for 'nourishing' or 'bringing up' – ie *educare*, not *educere* – but the idea of teachers 'leading out' pupils is too attractive to be dropped in favour of accuracy in Latin. (Perhaps the word 'education' could be replaced with 'eduction', to satisfy classicists *and* those teachers wishing to 'lead out' pupils.)

The idea of 'leading out' also fits with the idea that pupils can learn without teachers, just as musicians can perform without conductors: teachers/conductors are most needed when many pupils/musicians are performing at the same time in the same place, with the teaching/conducting rôle being one of co-ordination and interpretation. Other teachers see themselves as soloists, with the pupils as the audience. This idea fits with many popular views of teachers – as in Muriel Spark's *The Prime of Miss Jean Brodie*, and Christopher Rush's even harsher though rather less well-known *Last Lesson of the Afternoon: A Satire* (1994)

John Clare's book for history teachers describes differentiation in practice, and effectively promotes the idea of 'teacher as conductor':

> "When the history department at Greenfield began to address the issue of differentiation, our initial reaction was to try to simplify existing materials to cater for the less able pupils. Out of this grew a fund of teaching techniques which presented the key issues in a very clear and easy way. As time went on, we realised that the less able pupils were beginning to do better than pupils at the bottom of 'more able' classes. The harder lessons were leaving some 'able' pupils confused about issues which the less able were grasping firmly! The result was a change in the department's approach to differentiation. Instead of presenting different lessons depending on perceived ability, the department has adopted a 'how far can you go?' policy. All pupils start by studying the same issues in the same simple way. Once they have grasped the basic concepts, however, the facility exists for more able classes/pupils to go deeper into the subject. The programmes of study, therefore, provide opportunities for able pupils to 'go deeper' or to 'go further', both within each lesson and within each topic, whilst less able pupils will do as much as they can, but then move on to another subject. This approach will suit teachers of mixed ability classes. Differentiation by task is divisive, and not very successful. It is more effective to set open-ended tasks which can be tackled at different levels by pupils of different abilities, or series of tasks, where pupils of greater ability can progress further." (From Clare, 1995.)

The differentiated department: making the most of diversity, through mutual observation and support

"The best teachers are those who choose deliberately and inventively amongst a repertoire of learning activities, or who can judge when the pupils themselves can choose the strategies most likely to advance their learning"

Douglas Barnes, quoted in National Curriculum Council, 1991

The different skills and knowledge of teachers is often overlooked by school departments – even those who are well aware of differences between pupils. A general topic introduction can help ensure that each teacher is not having to repeat the same groundwork done by every other teacher, and that, on key issues (like the dating system used in the Muslim world, or the definition of 'revolution') the whole department is pulling together. This should save work, and helps in 'differentiation' as it applies to staff. Try to find topic introductions or similar guidance in your department, and if you cannot, then think about producing them yourselves. More important than this, think about your own prior learning and expertise, and your knowledge of different areas.

If teachers are unable to pool their expertise and ideas, it seems unreasonable to expect pupils to do group work with any enthusiasm. Barriers to mutual support – for pupils and teachers alike – are often caused by fear. Fear of being thought a 'poor' pupil/teacher, and fear of being thought a 'show off'. There are many ways of overcoming such barriers. It is important to give members of a group distinct tasks, so that one person cannot dominate the whole process. It is also useful to make the whole group responsible for the final product, so that no one person can be 'blamed' for the result. A simple technique, recommended by Tim Brighouse (Jones & Sparks, 1996, pages 3–4) is for one teacher to plan a lesson for another teacher, with the 'planner' observing. The subsequent discussion of the observed lesson is likely to be more productive as a result of the teachers' joint responsibility for the lesson. Less complex approaches to observation should still maintain the principle of mutuality: I'll show you mine if you show me yours.

Teachers may regularly work together in the same classroom, either team teaching (all too rare in cash-strapped times), or where one teacher is providing language or learning support. In these circumstances mutual observation and support is of course essential. Misunderstandings about rôles can cause a great deal of friction and resentment – especially for NQTs who are less likely to understand the precise rôles of different workers in the school. A simple way to help the relationship be effective is for the two teachers to draw up a 'contract' describing who should be responsible for what in the lesson. Other ways would be for either of the teachers to ask for the other's help. Asking for help, rather than giving advice or (even worse) orders, is generally the most productive approach for teachers at every level in the school.

Activity

1. Draw up a 'contract' that could be used for team teaching or for work with support teachers, or with classroom assistants (who may well not be teacher-trained), starting with the items in the table below **(Figure 4.1)**. An interesting spin-off from this exercise is to clarify what a 'solo' teacher can be expected to do in a classroom. It will be a long list.

A consequence of working effectively in teams is that you are more likely to work effectively in all situations. When a school is committed to education for all (including staff), it will create an ethos in which pupils and teachers are all working cooperatively to maximise individual and collective achievement. Close-knit teams, such as departments, can move from good practice to excellent practice, constantly raising the achievements of their pupils. More diverse groups, such as cross-curricular groups or homework centres, can feed off the ideas generated by different disciplines, creating imaginative links and thereby helping pupils see their education as much more than just a sum of its parts.

Teacher tasks			
Task	Teacher A – one of a team, or a subject specialist	Both teachers	Teacher B – one of a team, or a support teacher
Plan lesson to fit broader topic and subject plans			
Plan the lesson structure			
Produce materials specially for the lesson			
Organise the classroom, books, equipment, etc.			
Present the materials and activities of the lesson			
Work with individuals and groups of pupils on their learning tasks			
Ensure that pupils are on-task			
Set and explain homework task (and take in previous work)			
Assess work during the lesson; assess work after the lesson			
Complete lesson administration, including the register, report cards, day sheets, etc			
Other activities and responsibilities			

Figure 4.1   Team teaching contract

Teaching careers are now assumed to move through three stages, from proficient or competent teacher (the minimum or 'base line' level required of NQTs), through expert (or 'advanced skills') teachers, and on to leaders (subject leaders, school leaders, etc). There is some work later (in Chapter 8) on expertise and on being a head of department or subject leader, but it is worthwhile here starting to consider expertise:

- *Some might see expertise in terms of the* **number of skills** *demonstrated, so that an expert teacher could 'do more things' than a proficient teacher.*

- *Others might see expertise as referring to the* **level** *at which skills were demonstrated, so expert teachers could do the same things 'better'.*

- *A third view, which might be able to incorporate the other two views, would focus on expertise as a* **measure of progress** *beyond proficiency, for example, progress from being more dependent to being more independent.*

These three views, of breadth, depth, and progress, are tackled again in Chapter 8. The activity here attempts to point the way from the earlier consideration of dependence/independence to the later one of expertise.

Activity

See also page 24 on Vygotsky.

1. Fill in the table in **Figure 4.2** and then ask a colleague (a peer or a mentor) to fill the other half. Consider any differences of emphasis or disagreements. Do they point to further areas of development?

Expertise		
	Your own examples	**A colleague's view of your progress**
The best example of a new skill developed since starting teaching history.		
The best example of an improvement in a skill during the first year.		
The best example of progress during the first year.		

Figure 4.2 Examples of becoming expert

Flexible learning: avoiding the two-faced teacher

A teacher who pretends an interest in learning, but who in fact just wants to promote pupils' relatively thoughtless, passive, acceptance of given information, is being 'two-faced' about education. A history teacher with two faces may be saying "doing history is a good idea", and "pupils are only able to learn about history: they are unable to do history". The approach of 'flexible learning', popular (with that label) from the 1980s, attempts to overcome the dichotomy between doing and learning about history.

> "*Flexible learning is defined … as the creation of learning opportunities tailored to meet the needs of the learner. Components of this concept include learner autonomy and effectiveness, which are dependent in turn on the extent to which the process of learning is matched to the individual learner's needs for employment or otherwise, via negotiation and counselling and guidance*"

> Further Education Unit, 1983

Setting up a flexible learning system enables:

- *pupils to be better independent learners;*

- *teachers to be better teachers (differentiating work and giving responsibilities to pupils);*

- *all involved in the school to understand the learning process that much better.*

> "*By giving the student increasing responsibility for his or her own learning within a framework of support, teachers will find that, as well as learning the discrete school subjects, students will also develop a range of personal, social, information handling and learning-to-learn skills which considerably enhance personal effectiveness and help contribute to equalise and optimise opportunities for them*"

> *Trayers,* in TVEI, 1989

Teachers often overestimate the variety of the teaching techniques they use, just as they often underestimate the effectiveness of more pupil-centred techniques. Pupils themselves can 'put teachers right'.

Activity

1. Ask pupils you teach to describe your teaching techniques. This could be an informal chat, or a more organised survey (for example, at the end of a topic, or during a 'gap' in formal learning). Analyse their responses – and the reasons for their responses.

Every pupil must be involved in flexible learning. A philosophy of flexible learning would be neutralised if it ignored issues of equality of opportunity, especially with respect to access to resources. There are too many resource banks used by groups of pupils from a narrow range of courses, too many computers used by a narrow range of pupils, and too many teachers using a narrow range of resources.

Pupils should be involved in producing resources. Every teacher, too, must be involved, and of course must want to be involved – that is the rôle of good management. Flexible learning should incorporate materials for staff, and staff should be seen (by the students) studying – and enjoying it. Every room should be a 'resources centre' – teachers should understand the importance of display, layout, working atmosphere, and so on. Resource-based learning must be founded on the teachers and the pupils themselves.

Activity

1. When your teaching room is empty of pupils, look around and list all the materials produced by you, by pupils, and by colleagues in the school. Sometimes teachers feel that commercially produced posters and other resources are more impressive. However, the signs of flexible learning having gone on are the products of the learners themselves.

"Student responses to the [flexible learning] project questionnaires suggest, practically unanimously, that they prefer to be 'taught'. The reason they give is almost universally the same: that way they don't have to work so hard!"
(National Extension College, 1985).

DART activities: core experiences, differentiated work

DART work was stimulated by work on how children read-and-learn, particularly books like Lunzer and Gardner (1979).

DART activities are **Directed Activities Related to the Text**. For example, a piece of text might be explored by a class using carefully chosen exercises, in the same way that the class might 'explore' an historic site. It is this idea that helps many teachers realise how all pupils can do different (types and levels of) work, based on a common, central, text. Examples include:

- *sequencing;*
- *highlighting;*
- *matching sections;*
- *cloze;*
- *re-telling in different format.*

This allows reasonable access to a very difficult text which might otherwise be accessible to only a few of the pupils. DART techniques are at the core of any good use of stimulating resources – whether or not teachers know the term 'DART'.

There is a whole book of pictures, poems, and activities – Double Vision by Michael and Peter Benton (1990) – which is full of wonderful ideas for teachers of practically any subject.

A 'text', in this context, might be a picture. 'Busy' pictures, like those of Breughel, can be explored using stimulating questions, starting with "What is happening in this area of the picture?" Other interesting 'key' sources which can then be DARTed include maps, videos, artefacts (including videos/pictures of artefacts), songs, or even phrases/quotations (eg "*Liberté! Égalité! Fraternité!*"). Good classroom activities and display work can be generated from any of these.

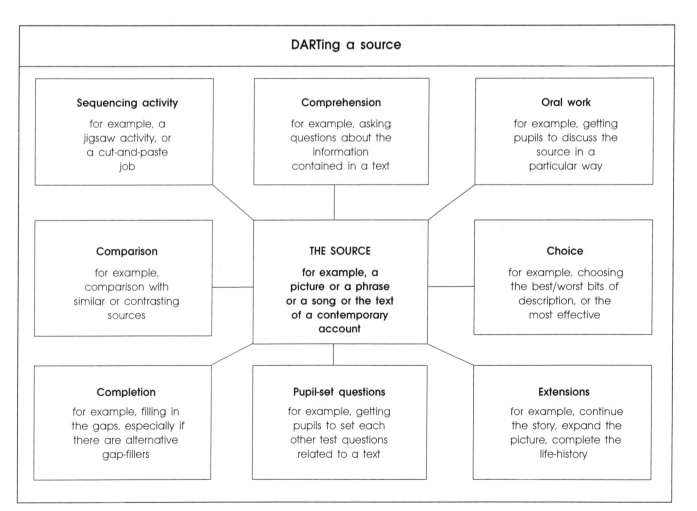

Figure 4.3   DART activities

Activity

1. Choose a 'source' from the exercise in Chapter 3 on the use of evidence **(Figure 3.2)**. Complete the diagram above **(Figure 4.3)**, explaining diverse ways of 'DARTing' the source. If the boxes are difficult to fill in, talk to other teachers in your department. If the source is a painting, you could consult the art department, if a song, the music department, etc.

   Whenever you use a key source, make use of the completed diagram to help you make the best use of it.

Homework: grabbing hold of the world and making it make sense for you

Practically every course for teachers either ignores homework altogether, or, at best, just mentions it. "Oh, and don't forget how important homework is" was how it was dealt with by one course. Clearly most schools put a great deal of effort into getting pupils to do homework, and getting teachers to set homework. It is used to complement classroom experiences, to promote strategies of independent learning, to finish off class work, to get homes/families involved in education, to research for GCSE coursework, and, no doubt, to fulfil many other functions including to punish children for their misdemeanours. However, much less time seems to be spent justifying, planning for, and supporting homework than is spent on class work.

Unfortunately, the literature on the subject is notable for the absence of evidence of:

- *what is done;*
- *how it is done;*
- *how homework (like class work) can be differentiated to meet the needs of different pupils;*
- *how homework can be organised to allow all pupils to achieve to their full potential.*

It is therefore worth working out good examples of homework tasks, including at least:

- *one oral/aural homework;*
- *one research homework;*
- *one 'learning' homework;*
- *one story or reading homework;*
- *one homework with cross-curricular significance;*
- *one homework involving pictures;*
- *one homework requiring interaction with the pupils' home;*
- *one problem-solving homework;*
- *one homework suited to school holidays.*

You might also want to think about how your teaching and your school would have to change if homework were abolished.

Note that this exercise avoids asking for specifically historical work: this is not accidental. Particular historical skills may be targeted in any of the categories of work. For example, in the completion/gap-filling exercise, the teacher may take out key historical concepts, in order to help pupils to clarify their meaning, or the teacher may just take out a random selection of words, in order to help the pupils focus on the text as a whole.

Think back to your own experience of being set homework when you were at school. What impression do you have of its purpose?

The fullest guide to the whole range of homework issues, covering all subjects in the National Curriculum, is the present author's book Homework and Study Support *(Stern, 1997). That also refers to such other research as had previously been done. DfEE (1998b) also addresses some of the issues.*

Activity

1. Look at the list of characteristics of school work and homework in **Figure 4.4**. Work out which apply to your history teaching and the work of the whole department and school.

2. Homework setting will only improve as teachers build on good practice. On the diagram below **(Figure 4.5)**, fill in examples of the best and worst homework tasks you feel you have set so far this year. Explain why you think the best was successful and why the worst failed. Then ask colleagues – perhaps at a departmental meeting. Then ask pupils – the most interesting source of evaluations.

School work	Homework
Everyone thinks it's a good idea.	Many people think it should be abolished (including several European countries).
Schools spend time planning it.	Schools spend little time thinking about it.
50% of pupils say they enjoy it.	2% of pupils say they enjoy it.
In an average week, a pupil spends 23 hours in school, or 91.7% of the amount expected.	In an average week, a pupil spends between one and three hours doing homework, or 30% of the amount expected.
Until the age of 16, pupils spend 15 000 hours in school, most of it studying.	Until the age of 16, pupils spend 125 000 hours at home, but only 0.25% of this time will be spent studying. Appropriate homework could add the equivalent of at least one additional year of full-time education.
There is little evidence of a connection between the amount of punishment in school and the amount of misbehaviour in school.	There is evidence of a connection between the amount of homework set and the amount of misbehaviour in school.
Pupils can learn better if: • they enjoy the work; • the work is challenging; • they have the facilities to complete the task; • they have someone to ask if they get stuck; • the work is, or is seen as, relevant, useful; • they understand the reasons for doing the work; • praise is given for work when done; • their friends are all doing or trying to do the work, too.	Homework: • is generally unenjoyable (98% of pupils); • is too easy or repetitive; • lacks facilities; • no-one regularly helps (54% of pupils); • no-one explains what it is for; • pupils rarely get praise for doing it; • is done away from friends (71% of pupils would work better with friends). • 57% of parents of primary pupils often help with their children's homework; • only 17% of parents of secondary pupils often help with their children's homework.
Lessons in school are generally pretty good. (84% of lessons were satisfactory or better, according to the OfSTED annual report published in February 1997.)	Homework: could do better. Parents, teachers and pupils all want homework to be worthwhile and interesting. If we all work together, homework can be what learning is at its best: grabbing hold of the world and making it make sense for you.

Figure 4.4 Comparing school work and homework

Best and worst homework task					
Best homework task	Why?	**Worst homework task**	Why?
As judged by yourself		As judged by yourself	
As judged by colleagues		As judged by colleagues	
As judged by your pupils		As judged by your pupils	

Figure 4.5   Homework survey

5
Resources in history

Aims

The aims of this Chapter are to:

- *help beginning teachers appreciate the amount and diversity of resources available to history teachers;*

- *improve skills in using resources to teach history;*

- *improve skills in organising collections of resources for history topics.*

Texts and textbooks as teachers and as sources: class sets, book boxes, and libraries

Becoming a more effective teacher is not simply about having lots of resources; an effective teacher will be one who makes the best use of resources already available. Books are good examples of this. They do not 'replace' teachers, as teaching is far more than giving out books and telling the children the page from which to work. Critically assessing books is the basis of the first three activities below, but later work focuses on how else books can be used.

Some people think it strange, but I get the impression that information in books 'seeps out': children seem to learn from books that they never seem to read. Perhaps they read books when we are not looking, or perhaps they get enough information from the writing and pictures on the cover. This mysterious quality of books should be remembered when evaluating books, in order to encourage pupils to go beyond 'obvious' features.

Farmer & Knight (1995) write of 'going beyond the text' as one of the twelve characteristics of effective history teaching. It is worth pointing out that pupils may read the same book in very different ways: an adventure story may be read for excitement by some pupils and for humour by others. History need not repeat itself: it can be read simultaneously as tragedy and comedy.

Activity

1. Work with pupils to assess class books (for themselves, and also for younger pupils), producing reviews explaining what the advantages and disadvantages are of each book. Surprisingly, over years of book-ordering, many teachers never ask the key readers – the pupils – to make comments on books, and treat comments (like 'this book is too complicated') as a sign of general disaffection rather than true criticism.

    Depending on the culture of the school and the interests of the pupils, it may be that a useful strategy would be to treat this exercise as one of producing an 'alternative guide'. University students may be involved in producing alternative prospectuses, and such guides are popular with prospective students. The same will be true for many school students.

2. From your point of view as a teacher, work on what text books *have* and what they *do not have* (for your pupils), in terms of:

    - *narrative qualities;*

    - *varied sources;*

    - *types of exercise;*

    - *congruence with the department's scheme of work or exam syllabus.*

    Then, use this information to inform your planning. No book is likely to be complete, so your other input to lessons should stress those elements not covered so well in the books. Too many teachers say "we've got the wrong books" in a tone suggesting that no change is possible in the way they teach, to complement whatever strengths the available books have.

3. Make a booklist, referring to:

    - *school and public libraries;*

    - *HEI libraries;*

    - *TES and history journal reviews;*

    - *current bookshops.*

Using Higher Education Institutions should be particularly stressed. NQTs are likely to have good contacts, from their period of training. HEI and other libraries can be visited, and may also be accessed using the Internet. Publishers, too, are now likely to have their own sites.

This list should be available for the whole department, so that, should money be available, your preferences can affect the department's choice. Many departments may be committed to a single textbook or series of textbooks as class sets, but will be quite prepared, perhaps on your recommendation, to buy single copies of books you would like to have available.

National Council for Educational Technology (1990) is interesting on partnership between teachers and librarians.
It is also useful to consult directories of free or cheap resources, such as Brown's Goldmine (1995).

Once you have done this 'critical' work, it is worth talking to the librarian. Or rather, listening to the librarian. Librarians are the people most concerned with the management of learning resources, and yet teachers often regard them as no more than a person to go "shh". One of the tasks that teachers and librarians can do together is to prepare a 'book box'. This is a box of a wide range of books, and perhaps other resources, from the library and departmental stock, covering a single topic. The box is most useful for project work by pupils, where different pupils will need resources beyond the basic class text, but where a lot of the work needs to be done during lesson time. Negotiating with the librarian, about the possibility of using book boxes, is a useful way to explain your aims as a history teacher, and to get to know the aims of the librarian, too.

Activity

1. Plan for, prepare, use, and evaluate a **book box** or similar method of making use of diverse texts with pupils.

Eg Deary (1996a) or Deary (1996b).

Pupils' understanding of books is not limited to school textbooks. Popular books, such as the *Horrible Histories* of Terry Deary, or part-works from publishing houses like Marshall Cavendish, are sometimes more familiar to pupils than the books they are using every day in school.

Activity

1. Work with a class – probably a Year 7 class – to create a book of a topic. The book should be designed for a purpose, such as teaching pupils at a feeder primary school.

There is a whole educational movement centred on the making of books. The Freinet movement sees the production process as well as the intellectual process as vital.

Stories, songs and pictures: narrative drive and imaginative leaps

Academics often divide history into **pre-critical** and **critical history**. (Paddy Walsh (in Lee, 1992) writes about this tradition, in a most compact guide to debates within history in education.) Pre-critical history incorporates much of the 'fiction' in which there is an attempt to describe events over time. The possibility of using such works in lessons should be welcomed. It is precisely the ability of fiction to engage readers and to make sense of complex situations that can help history teachers. The 'narrative drive' of good stories can pull pupils through historical periods. Songs and pictures, too, are able to 'grab' pupils, and, especially those from periods of lower literacy levels, often had the specific function of passing on a community's version of its own history.

Claire (1996) includes excellent guidance, aimed at Key Stages 1 and 2, for developing pupils' family histories, and for using stories to support the teaching of history. Many of the suggestions can be adjusted to suit Key Stage 3. One of the best books of short, readable, stories is Jackson (1994): although designed for primary assemblies, the stories could be used in many contexts in secondary schools.

Perfetti et al (1995) say: "*To learn history is to learn a story. To understand history as a nonexpert is to know the story. There is more to both learning and understanding history than this, of course. We claim merely that what one knows includes a story*". The authors go on to investigate the relationship between stories and explanations, and much else besides. Maddern (1992) goes beyond this to describe opportunities for storytelling at historic sites. Linking stories with sites and objects is clearly a good way of helping pupils appreciate the multiplicity of types and qualities of historic sources. However, storytelling, like charity, begins at home.

Starting with the fictions held by pupils and their communities, it is worth stressing the value of building on the varied traditions held by the people most directly involved in the school. In a school serving a relatively stable and less diverse community, the traditions held by members of that community are more likely to be complementary, and closely related to the places and people familiar to all at the school. This can make for a powerful sense of local history. A school serving a more diverse, changing, community will be more likely to contain enormously varied traditions. In this case, a greater sense of the variety of possible lifestyles and perspectives can be seen. Beginning teachers, often working in schools in unfamiliar areas, should value opportunities to make use of these sources, for their own sakes as well as for the sake of developing more effective history resources.

Activity

1. Develop a **story-bank** from the people in and connected to the school. This could be on a particular theme, or it could try to reflect the diverse experiences of pupils, or it could be simply all the stories available. Themes might include stories of schools, or of wars, or of childhood, or of magical happenings. The story-bank could be aimed at younger children, as pupils often enjoy collecting, and telling, stories to younger people. Good sources of stories are older members of the community, and, within the school, non-teaching staff. Perhaps this is because both groups may have a stronger oral than literary tradition, compared with the more academic and literary traditions from which teachers are more commonly drawn. If pupils have home-languages other than English, it is particularly valuable to collect stories in original languages and to try to get these translated. Mother-tongue and English teaching can both be enhanced by this process.

   Connecting story-telling to history is the increasingly popular pursuit of 'alternative history', variously described as 'possible history' or (occasionally less charitably) 'science fiction'. Ferguson (1997) contains many attempts to tackle 'what ifs'. Pupils, perhaps more than professional historians, often find this approach exciting. Alternative history is also referred to in Chapter 1, above.

2. Whatever sources and types of stories, try to fit these into the history curriculum. They may fit easily, as would stories of the Second World War, or they may be used as examples of alternative perspectives on an event, or more-or-less reliable sources of evidence, and so on.

Beyond the pupils' own traditions, you should of course be aware of and make use of wider literary traditions. This includes the literary works available in the school, and available to pupils outside school. Writing of the period being studied has a special value. NQTs should allow for work on such texts, and not be too worried about archaic language, as long as the work is tackled with care. For example, extracts from *Sir Gawain and the Green Knight*, written in the 14th century, can make a lively class reading to accompany work on castles or on the medieval period in general.

The works of Shakespeare, and those attributed to Homer, are excellent examples of fictions-telling-histories, and are to be recommended for (careful) use in history lessons. Historians can study the use of authors' works, too, as in Strobl (1997), which tackles the use of Shakespeare by leaders of the Nazi Germany.

The National Curriculum Council published a guide: *Historical novels to support the teaching of history at Key Stage 3*, with 30 pages of recommended texts. It is prefaced with the warning that "*teachers must make it clear that novels are fictional and do not constitute evidence about the past. Pupils will, therefore, need to compare information from historical fiction with evidence from historical sources and with accounts found in the text books*". This may seem a little extreme a warning, with *Huckleberry Finn*, *The Scarlet Pimpernel*, a modern version of *El Cid*, and other 'classics', at least, surely qualifying as 'evidence', even if the evidence is to be treated with great care.

Activity

1. Work with the school librarian and/or the English department, to produce a school reading list of fiction available for Key Stage 3 and Key Stage 4 history. This may even be extended to Key Stage 5. It is important to develop lists from what is available, so that pupils can expect to find any books you recommend.

   Producing booklists is useful for your personal and professional development, and complements the work described in Chapter 2 and elsewhere in the book.

2. A useful follow-up activity would be get pupils to search their own houses and/or local libraries and/or the Internet, to create lists of fiction available outside the school library.

3. The third stage of this work would be to develop lists of books to be bought by the school, and if pupils have been involved in producing such a list, that should give it more weight.

In many cultures, songs have been used to pass on history. In the USA to this day, country & western music has chronicled key events, with a simple, open, narrative style. Often more oblique historical references are made in older songs, at a time when the penalties for being on the 'wrong' side might have been harsher. Scottish Jacobite songs may have lyrics referring

"God grant that Marshal Wade
May by thy mighty aid
Victory bring.
May he sedition hush
And like a torrent rush
Rebellious Scots to crush,
God save the King."

Oh What a Lovely War *was*
developed by Joan Littlewood and
others, and made into a film in
1969. There are many books of
songs of the period, with perhaps
the best one being Oh! It's a Lovely
War: Songs, Ballads and Parodies
of the Great War, *published by EMI*
Music in 1978. The Imperial War
Museum produces cassettes of
songs of the First World War, from
recordings made at the time.

to a lover, in fact referring to the Bonnie Prince. Nationalist songs in general make for lively history. Indeed, to complement Jacobite songs, a teacher might use the verse of the National Anthem sung in England in 1745.

The topic 'The Making of the United Kingdom' yields many more songs, from all the areas that went to make up the United Kingdom. Similarly, the First World War produced almost as much popular song as it did verse. Work can be done on the apparent aims of the songs, as well as on the details of the content.

Activity

1. Work with the school's music department (or anyone else interested in songs) to put together a song-guide to certain periods in history. The musical play *Oh What a Lovely War*, may be ambitious, but it has proved popular with schools since the 1970s.

Pictures are excellent sources for history teachers, with good quality reproductions of many useful pictures very easily available, and galleries or picture collections in palaces and other historic buildings relatively easy to visit from anywhere in the UK. Whether looking at Elizabethan portraits, or 20th century photographs, work can be done questioning the pictures as sources, looking for symbols, the significance of the perspective (where 'perspective' is, for once, meant literally), propaganda purposes, and so on.

Activity

1. Where a picture is available to the teacher, a valuable exercise is to get pupils to play the 'stolen picture' game. Having studied the life of Queen Elizabeth 1, pupils could be told of a portrait that was painted, but had been stolen. What would they put into the empty frame? What sort of clothes would she be wearing, would there be references to any key events in her reign? And so on. After the pupils had made their pictures, the portrait might be 'found' again, and the pupils could compare their efforts to the real thing. (A more recent example might be the creation, after her resignation, of a coat of arms for Margaret Thatcher.)

Fictional stories, songs and pictures then can help develop pupils' sense of narrative structure, and should also help improve their communication skills in general. Making imaginative leaps is valuable in many areas of education (and life), and creativity is a quality too often underplayed in schools. History teachers can learn much from teachers of English, music, and art, for example. English teachers will often stimulate creative writing by giving pupils the first part of a story, asking the pupils to finish the story. History teachers can do the same, speculating about unfamiliar series of events. Stimulating extended prose, the teacher can give the first sentence of each paragraph of an essay to pupils, asking them to complete the paragraphs. This is usefully done in class, using an OHP, but can also be done for homework. Similarly, time-lines can be turned into narratives (or vice versa), as a way of enhancing the learning of each style of communication.

This exercise is particularly useful
for pupils starting GCSE and A
Level courses, where extended
writing is central to the formal
assessment procedures.

There is a whole book of 'writing
frames' (Lewis & Wray, 1996),
giving ideas on how teachers can
set up such activities.

Information and communication technology and history: byting back

NQTs have been expected to develop and demonstrate various ICT skills in recent PGCE courses. However, many may still find ICT daunting. Developing its use can be difficult in the first year of teaching, when confidence in the more basic school routines needs to be built up, and the prospect of working with (often temperamental) technology is simply too much. Here, work is recommended on the use of ICT in ways that will make life easier for NQTs, and not (it is hoped) increase anxiety levels. Beginning teachers already more confident in the use of ICT could still benefit from considering the issues covered here, and might think about how their skills and confidence could be used in the department.

The first point to be made is that pupils will use ICT, especially (currently) word-processing, the Internet, and CD-Roms, both to research and to present their work. Teachers who limit their ICT thinking to what they can do with a class-full of pupils miss the point: given the amount of access (in homes, in school, in libraries, and elsewhere) beyond the classroom, teachers need to think about interesting ways to manage and utilise the ICT work of their pupils.

The title 'byting back' is used in
Stern (1998), a specialist
publication on ICT. That book, and
this one, refer to ICT primarily as
computers, although the
government currently define ICT
as including videos, radio and so
on (see DfEE 1998a). Chapter 8 of
Haydn et al (1997) is an excellent
account using the broader
definition of ICT.

ICT can break down barriers, and allow pupils to find huge quantities of information, well-presented, at the touch of a few keys. Yet the second point to be made is that changing the technology does not thereby change the information, and certainly does little in itself to change the use to which information is put. Teachers must be aware of the need to develop historical skills and understanding, when dealing with pupils who have ICT access, just as when dealing with pupils using books. Terry Haydn (in *Teaching History 86*, 1997) writes about the exercise of fitting labels to a picture of a Roman soldier, and how the technology of CD-Roms may change the quality of the pictures, but fails in itself to make the exercise any more valuable in developing historical understanding or skills.

A third point concerns the availability of computers, and the consequent equal opportunities issues for teachers. Over 25% of UK homes currently have computers, and this figure will inevitably rise over the next few years. Although there is much debate about the division between 'computer technology rich' and 'computer technology poor' homes, most schools and local libraries enable good ICT work to be done by all pupils, as long as a flexible-enough approach is taken.

Activity

1. Set up a research-based piece of work for pupils, and divide the labour, amongst the class, so that some are expected to use ICT techniques, whilst others might use books or other sources of information.

2. Set up rules governing the use of information from ICT. For example, where CD-Rom encyclopaedias are used, pupils should be asked to do more than print out extracts. A '25% originality' rule is useful – ie 25% of any work produced using such encyclopaedias must be commentary, analysis, or other original work by the pupil.

3. Set up systems by which pupils with better ICT access (especially those with computers at home) make their advantage work to the benefit of pupils (and teachers) with worse access. For example, such pupils might produce guides to particular topics, from ICT sources, either for their peers or for younger pupils. The skill of selection (of the most valuable material) is a vital one to develop for all historians. They might also review available CD-Roms (general encyclopaedic titles as well as specialist historical ones) or historical games and simulations.

It would be reasonable to expect equivalent contributions from pupils with poorer access to ICT. For example, such pupils might be expected to produce guides based on books, journals, or television/ video sources.

4. Pool useful websites. A subject like history has a huge amount of information on the Internet. Having pupils, teachers, and others interested in the systems produce address-lists for the most useful sites would help teachers and pupils alike.

   Such an exercise might be a useful one to be done during staff development time. A popular website, at the time of writing, is http://www.liv.ac.uk/~evansjon/humanities/history/history.html. There is little point in listing many sites, as, currently, sites and addresses change so quickly.

As John Fines points out "each act of selection rejects a vast quantity of other material" (Fines, 1984).

There has been such rapid change in ICT over the last few years, it seems likely that teachers will never be ahead of the keener pupils, but teachers who ignore ICT altogether are likely to feel more and more lost. Your first years should at least be full of curiosity and openness. Dean (1995) Chapter 3 and Nichol (1995) Chapter 3, provide general accounts of uses of ICT in history. Though any such guide will quickly become technically dated, the principles can be applied to new situations. Page 52 of Dean's book is a checklist for evaluating software.

Incidentally, a use of computers that is likely to increase, is the technology enabling a computer monitor image to be projected onto a screen. White boards and OHPs may become a thing of the past, if the cost of the projectors becomes more realistic.

Wonderful worksheets

Becoming a better history teacher includes all kinds of sophisticated changes, but a teacher who fails to produce effective worksheets for pupils is missing a key characteristic of the profession. There are two approaches to worksheets outlined here:

Tolley et al (1996b) Chapter 5 has a guide to worksheets and other resources, complementing this guide.

Nichol (1995) and Dean (1995) both have examples of worksheets to be used and/or evaluated.

- teachers can try to produce **better** worksheets;
- and they can try to produce **wonderful** worksheets.

How to make better worksheets is easily taught but too rarely learned. It is an insult to pupils to give them scrappy, unclear, badly reproduced worksheets, that often break all the presentation rules pupils are expected to follow.

1. **'Better' rules** include the following:

   - Give the worksheet a border of at least half an inch (preferably more), so that nothing is lost in reproduction;
   - Use a clear typeface (where the work is word-processed) with a font size of at least 12 points;
   - Avoid typefaces that look impressive but are unreadable, including most 'pseudo-handwriting' fonts and most 'historic' fonts;
   - For younger pupils or those with reading difficulties, and those literate in a first language using a different alphabet (such as Bengali, Russian, or Japanese), think about how the letters 'a' and 'g', in particular, are formed, and try to be consistent in all worksheets and other school documents.

2. Follow the same **rules of presentation** you would expect of pupils:

   - Underline titles;
   - Avoid using block capitals for headings or important words. Block capitals may look impressive to you, but they are harder to read (especially for those with reading difficulties) as they create oblong-shaped words thereby reducing the distinctiveness of the shape of the word;

   In this book, the main text is justified: adult readers are less likely to find this a problem, though.

   - Oblong-shaped text, too (ie justified, or aligned at both ends of the line), is also harder to read than text aligned only at the left;
   - Text at 45° angles would in general be unacceptable in pupils' work, and does nothing to help them read worksheets.

3. **Pictures help focus readers**. The use of simple icons, such as a 'book' icon for sections to be read, and a 'pen' icon where pupils are to write, can improve worksheets and are easily available. It is not necessary to have a huge library of images to use, as a small number of useful items is likely to cover most requirements. If photographs or other pictures are to be used, see how they reproduce, before using them, otherwise you will end up having to tell your class "that darker bit is a tank and the smudge in front of it is probably a soldier, but it could be a horse".

4. **Instructions are needed** to help pupils through worksheets. Being explicit is advantageous. A worksheet with quotations and questions on it might be prefaced "Read the three quotations below. Write the title of the worksheet in your exercise book, then answer questions 1 to 5. Remember to write your answers in full sentences. Try to finish all the questions during this lesson".

5. **Avoid questions** of the form "Why did Henry VIII come into conflict with the Pope, what effect did this have on his reign, and what sort of evidence is available to back your view?" One question should require one answer, so questions on worksheets should be written in short sentences.

Colour-coding worksheets, using the same colour for every 'task' sheet, and the same colour for every 'test' sheet, can help pupils clarify their work more easily.

6. When it comes to **reproducing the worksheet,** do not accept poor copies. Making fewer, better quality, worksheets is better than rushing to produce a large quantity of unreadable ones. Using coloured paper, if the colour is a light one, can make worksheets more distinctive and easier to identify by pupils and teachers.

Making wonderful worksheets (let's call them WWs) includes following the 'better worksheets' advice. It also involves thinking about exactly what pupils might need in certain circumstances. It is worth picking out a sub-topic, or an issue, of concern to the whole department, and try to produce a WW to meet the needs identified:

- A WW will be **self-sustaining**. That is, it will stimulate (perhaps inspire) a large quantity of good work with minimal teacher-input. It will also be well differentiated, taking account of the various skills and aptitudes of all the pupils who will use it.

- Most WWs contain some **stimulus material** – perhaps a text or a picture – with questions helping pupils to 'get into' the material, and activities related to the stimulus. For example, work on life in the 16th century might use Shakespeare's 'seven ages' speech from As You Like It, with exercises getting pupils to understand, order and select information, and activities involving comparisons of descriptions in the text with possible 20th century descriptions.

- "Could I have a copy of that?" (if asked) is a sign of a WW, whether the question is asked by pupils or teachers. This may be said on first view. It is interesting how many WWs are 'striking': more than just clear, the message seems to jump off the page. This may be a result of simplicity, or of completeness. Like a great painting, a WW will draw the audience in. Such a quality is easier to spot than to describe, of course, but once spotted, it should be replicated whenever possible.

Farmer & Knight (1995) have examples of worksheets and other materials, based on several of the most common topics in Key Stage 3 history.

A full version is given of this example in Stern (1995) pages 42–44.

Activity

1. Choose a small selection of your own or your department's worksheets and improve them. Use the guide, above, to help you. Once you have done this, give the old and new worksheets to pupils, and ask them which they prefer, and why.

2. Ask teachers and pupils what their best-ever worksheet is, and why. Use this information to produce at least one WW during your NQT year. Again, once you have done this, test it out on colleagues and pupils.

People as sources: pupils, teachers, families, and beyond

History is human, and making use of people as sources will help pupils understand this. We are all 'bearers' or 'inheritors' or perhaps 'products' of history, so, as a new history teacher, you have a particularly handy resource to use with pupils. 'We' includes the pupils themselves, teaching staff (in all departments), non-teaching staff (sadly ignored by many teachers), families, friends, experts (such as staff at museums or historic sites) and everyone else. It is not that pupils should expect all people to have answers to questions like "When did Rome become a republic?". Rather, they should be able to ask people their views (or 'perspectives') on issues, and on ways in which the course of history may have influenced them.

We should encourage visitors, but avoid the approach known as 'grab a granny', as warned in Parsons in Teaching History 84 (1996). *Treating visiting speakers with respect means more than respecting their lives, it means connecting their lives to the lives of pupils. The psychologist Phil Salmon, writing about old age, says that "giving to others from one's own heritage of experience surely means more than telling grandchildren stories about the past. Experience itself usually cannot be communicated, or even felt, from cold. It can be called up only through personal encounters in the present with something of the same kind" (Salmon, 1985).*

Activity

1. Describe a lesson or homework task for which you asked (or will ask) pupils to talk to each other about a topic, to help them develop their views on that topic. Perhaps the pupils could rôle-play then record a conversation between a 17th century medically skilled woman (such as a midwife) and her 'customer'. Or they might, for example, interview each other about how they would have responded to being called-up after 1916 in World War One. This should be additional to forms of peer work such as mutual marking, or simple group work. There are many ways of pupils supporting each other, including mutual marking, group work tasks, and research involving a division of labour. Keith Topping (1988) has written about various forms of peer tutoring, and such work is becoming much more popular in the 1990s. Here, however, the task is looking at pupils using each other as sources or to rôle-play historical figures.

2. Describe an out-of-class task involving talking to adults in the school. For example, set up survey work on changes in education during the last 40 years, or perhaps interview adults about last week's news, in order to investigate the ways in which people are selective in their memories of (even recent) events.

    The history of the school itself, told by pupils and staff, past and present, is a topic mentioned again in the 'environments' section (see below p 54) and the English Heritage book.

The Parent's Charter (described in Tolley et al, 1996a, p 10) refers to parental engagement.

3. Describe an out-of-school task involving talking to adults at home. For example, as an introduction to a revolutions topic, get the pupils to ask five adults what the word 'revolution' means to them. When working on the use of photographs as evidence, you might ask pupils to collect holiday photographs from home, and talk about the holidays where they were taken. (The smiles on most holiday photographs are useful when talking about bias in evidence.)

   This stresses the value of people as holders of opinions and perspectives, rather than as (primarily) holders of 'facts'. It also allows families to help with homework, without feeling obliged to be 'experts'.

See also the 'teacher interviews' described in Chapter 2.

4. Describe a class or school-visit activity in which pupils organise an interview of an 'expert' on a topic. A visiting speaker, or staff at a site visited, are likely to welcome curiosity, and a chance to explain what they know and believe.

5. Show how much you value people as resources, by displaying in the classroom photographs of classes you teach, pupils on visits, speakers visiting the school, and so on. Braver teachers may even display their own holiday snaps (taken in suitably 'historic' settings, of course) or other family pictures.

Places as sources: using environments, starting with the classroom

Few NQTs will organise many trips in their first year, but they can feel happy in the knowledge that more visits can be organised in subsequent years.

It has been said already (at the start of this Chapter) that more effective teachers may not possess more resources, but they are likely to regard more things and people as resources. Environments illustrate this well. Some history teachers complain of how far away the nearest 'historic site' is, or how difficult it is organising trips to such sites. Others, however, will make use of whatever sites are available, starting with the school itself, and working outwards from there. A good, full, use of the local environment combines the advantages of helping you develop as a teacher and helping your process of induction into the school and its community. And it can be pleasurable, and only a little cruel, to ask a distracted pupil, who is staring out of the window, to describe as a historian aspects of the view seen through that window.

Croall (1992) and Griffin & Eddershaw (1994) are both excellent, practical, texts on the whole range of uses of locality. Purkis (1993) is a specialist book on using the school buildings themselves to teach history. The second and third of these books address architectural issues (ie ways of dating a building), issues of records, and memories of participants.

The classroom is the best place to start. It can be used in many ways. When working on the development of world trade, materials used in the classroom can illustrate the diverse origins of materials and products, or changes over time. When working on feudal and other systems in which social status is central, the shape or arrangement of the classroom, or even the size and comfort of the teacher's chair and desk (compared with the pupils' chairs and desks), can be used as interesting illustrations. When looking at evidence and how it can be used, classrooms can be 'read', looking for evidence of the work (or even just the presence) of different staff and groups of pupils. Not all NQTs, of course, will be given a classroom in which to teach most or all their lessons: this is sometimes seen as a privilege of established teachers.

Such work on classrooms is useful as a way of encouraging work on display in the classroom. If there is little evidence of the presence of pupils, or of historians, then the classroom is being under-used.

Beyond the classroom, the school site as a whole is worth investigating, including (to use the title of a book of local history) 'the fields beneath'. Many schools will have been built on land whose previous use is well known to older local residents, who may have interesting stories to tell. The sense of a place having a long history, affecting its current status, is well worth developing in pupils, as long as it gets beyond anecdote, and the characteristics of the environment itself are considered. The position of a school at the top of a hill might indicate the community was wealthier, for example, as the water might be cleaner: but speculation is not enough, and further research will be needed to confirm this.

Real history is more important than mere surface features. That is why visitors to the north of Belgium are almost as likely to visit fields (sites of First World War battles), as the more obviously 'historic' cities of Brugge or Gent. It is the power of the war narrative that draws visitors to the fields, rather than some objective characteristics of the sites themselves.

Activity

1. For each history topic taught during the year, write a description of how you will use (or have used) the classroom, the school environment, and/or the local community by completing the table below in **Figure 5.1**. These environments may be used as evidence related directly to the topics, or as comparisons with evidence more directly related.

Moving out from the school and the local environment, the new teacher will need to develop skills of organising and working on longer field trips. An understanding of regulations is vital if a school trip is to be successful, and yet an understanding of the educational value of a trip is equally important if the trip is to be anything more than an exercise in logistics. The personal qualities of the teacher might determine whether logistical or educational issues need more development in the beginning years. Here, the logistics will be mentioned first, as failing to appreciate them can lead to legal, professional and even financial, rather than just pedagogical, difficulties. The activities described below are valuable whether or not a visit is arranged in the NQT year: in fact, doing the activities before thinking about arranging a visit is probably the best option.

Activity

1. Each school and Local Authority will have its own regulations and procedures relating to visits. Find out what they are: they will often be in the staff handbook.

   Following regulations is worth doing for more than a sense of obedience: insurance and other forms of financial and professional protection are likely to depend on regulations having been followed.

2. Having found out what the regulations are, produce a set of key documents that might be needed for any trip. (Use the structures in **Figure 5.2** if these help.) This should include a letter to families, asking permission for the visit to go ahead. There should also be a list of rules and guidance for pupils on the day, including:

   - instructions on timings during the day;
   - footwear and wet-weather clothing;
   - food needed;
   - money that might be spent;
   - writing equipment;
   - the code of behaviour (and perhaps sanctions) on the trip;
   - where to go and who to contact if lost;
   - the telephone number of the school in case of emergency.

   Finally, there is the information sheet you will need to leave with staff who remain in the school – including how they might contact you.

3. The third task is to make a list for yourself. This may include a list of things for you to do, and, equally important, a list of things to take. Things to take include:

   - spare pens and paper;
   - tissues (which are always useful);
   - telephone numbers (including the site to be visited, the coach company, the school, etc);
   - registers;
   - maps.

The current legislation on health and safety issues is worth further study. As well as information produced by unions and professional associations, documents such as Stock (1991) and Spackman (1991) may prove useful.

It may seem strange to a new teacher that there is any need to list such apparently obvious things for pupils, but the school and the outside world are so different, and the pupils are so used to following quite different rules in and out of school, that being explicit is essential.

Using the school to teach history		
	How is the school used already?	How might the school be used in the future?
Classroom		
Whole school environment		
Local community		

Figure 5.1   Using the school to teach history

Ask more experienced teachers if there is anything else to put on your list, and use the same list on more than one visit, adjusting it as your experience widens. Visits will involve more than one member of staff, and it is helpful to work out in advance a division of labour between the participants. (Again, use **Figure 5.2** if it helps.)

Preparation should be done by the teacher who is going on the visit: not as obvious as it seems, as the present author has discovered when, relying on maps and worksheets produced by his predecessors, he found that new roads had been built in the town visited, helpful landmarks had been demolished, and museums had rearranged their exhibits.

The logistics of the visit and the educational value are tied together, and the first educational rule might just as well be the last logistical rule: prepare in advance what you want out of the visit. The preparation is needed to make the most out of a visit in the context of the courses being taught, and to make the most of the site being visited. It is during the first year of working in an area that preparation work of this kind is most valuable. Therefore, as above, it is worth doing such preparatory work even if you arrange no visits: the work will be excellent grounding for the second and subsequent years of teaching.

Is there someone willing to look after a pupil who is ill – including travel sickness that can spoil an otherwise perfect visit? Can someone afford the time to wait behind for a lost pupil, should that be needed, and take the pupil back on a later train or bus?

Activity

1. Find out from the school and other sources what visits might suit each topic taught during the year. Large museums and other popular sites are of course worth listing, but it may be helpful to work on smaller or less well-known places which may be less busy or booked-up. Museums themselves often recommend limiting visits to about an hour, as the atmosphere created to preserve exhibits is often rather tiring for people. In an hour, good work could be done in the smallest of museums. Make sure you consider visits to places that might be of interest to teachers of other subjects: a medieval church may appeal to the RE department, an exhibition of portraits to the art department, an industrial museum to the technology department, and so on. Joint visits may spread costs and work, as well as improve the quality of the learning at the site and the reputation of the history department. Complete **Figure 5.3** below and use it as a basis for discussions with history colleagues and teachers from other departments.

Any visit will be 'in the present', of course. The television series of the Cadfael stories could not be filmed in Shrewsbury Abbey (too many modern bits) or anywhere else in Shrewsbury (too much traffic): it was filmed, apparently, in Hungary, which resembles medieval England rather more. Similarly, Mozart's Vienna, in the film Amadeus, *was filmed in Prague.*

2. Pick out from **Figure 5.3** the places you are most likely to use for school trips, and arrange to visit them yourself. Even if you have visited the place before, perhaps as a child or as a student, visit it again with a 'teacher's eye'. Work out if there is somewhere to eat packed lunches, where the boys' and girls' toilets are, whether the shop can cope with 30 customers, and of course what the site is like for a visit by historians. If possible, try to meet as many as possible of the people involved in running the site, especially the education officer if there is one. Try also to talk to the curators and people running the shops or canteens, who may have particularly useful advice to give.

There may well be a shop with guides to the site, and perhaps stories about the site, which may prove invaluable for the teacher.

3. Pick out an even narrower selection of trips – perhaps just one or two – consulting with your department. Using all available resources (including departmental worksheets if there has been a trip there in the past), plan how a visit could be prepared for educationally. What information and exercises should the pupils be familiar with in order to make the most of the site? How are they to record what they see and do on the visit, so that follow-up work can be done? What will be done in class after the visit, to build on the trip? What, too, will be done in the school to describe the trip to others (such as displays, notices in newsletters, etc)?

Photographs and videos are useful evidence, but writing and drawing, done by pupils during the day, will also be needed. Memories are generally insufficient.

Objects as sources: using artefacts

There is no simple division between those things referred to as objects (or artefacts) and elements of environments, texts, or displays. However, the aim of this Chapter is not to settle arguments about definitions, but to encourage effective use of resources. Here, artefacts are taken to be easily transportable non-text resources. Using artefacts is familiar to most secondary pupils from their earlier schooling. Primary schools often have well-established procedures for pupils bringing objects to school and talking about them. Primary classrooms, too, often have imaginatively organised displays of artefacts related to particular themes. Secondary schools,

See Durbin et al (1990). This is a fine book of ideas on quizzing objects.

Farmer & Knight (1995, pages 43–44), point out how unfortunate it is that artefacts are used so much more in Key Stages 1 and 2 than 3 or 4.

Documentation for history field trips

History trip: letter home

Use headed paper if available.

Include the date of the letter and the date by which a reply is required.

Include the pupil's name, and address the letter to the parent/carer. If you know the name, use it, but don't assume it is the same as the pupil's name. If you are not sure, start 'Dear parent/guardian/carer'.

Text:

History trip: pupil guidance

Aims of the trip:

Timing of the day:

How to make the trip successful:

In case of emergency:

History trip: sheet for staff

Pupils going:

Timing of the day:

In case of emergency:

History trip: reminders

To be organised prior to the trip:

To be organised on the day of the trip:

To be organised after the trip:

Figure 5.2   Documentation for history field trips

apparently more concerned with text, and using classrooms for several classes a day, often ignore such techniques. It would be to a beginning teacher's advantage to visit and observe work done in primary schools, especially when artefacts (of the pupils, collected by the teacher, or on loan from museums) are being used.

Activity

1. As part of the induction programme, arrange to work with a primary school. If possible, offer to work with them on a history topic, making use of artefacts. It may be possible for you to take some secondary pupils with you, or to get some of your pupils to do preparatory work.

Working with artefacts can help pupils grasp difficult concepts, and can help bring alive all kinds of topics. It is most valuable to develop ways of interrogating objects (how is it made? what is it made from? how is it used? etc), and ways of getting pupils to observe them closely (for example through careful drawing), and other ways of linking them to their history. Thomas Hood's *Song of the Shirt* is a fine example of a literary attempt to explain the labour in the simplest of objects. Work on apparently ephemeral artefacts can demonstrate the way in which the significance of objects can change according to circumstances. Half a return ticket for a train journey may seem insignificant, but if it was for the day of the 1913 Derby and was found in Emily Davidson's trunk, after she died, the ticket might seem more important.

*"O! men with sisters dear,
O! men with mothers and wives!
It is not linen you're wearing out,
But human creatures' lives!"
(Thomas Hood, Song of the Shirt, published in Punch, Christmas 1843.)*

Clearly, teachers will benefit from collecting artefacts, for themselves or for the school, and from working on ways of using artefacts in the classroom. Some teachers are wary of using artefacts, however, because of fears of how the objects may be treated. It is a perfectly reasonable fear, as objects may be precious or sacred to some, yet insignificant to others. The activity, below, is intended to address this issue.

Work on evidence related to the 'Suffragette Derby' is in Hinton (1990) pages 60-61.

Activity

1. Describe an activity with pupils on objects precious to them. The activity is perhaps best suited to younger pupils, in order to develop early respectful attitudes to artefacts. The activity might for example be of the 'show and tell' style, or work on time capsules (popular when working on the Egyptians, and therefore often done in Key Stage 2). It may also be in the form of a quiz or interrogation of the object, and this may bring up important issues of authenticity.

RE departments often use religious artefacts in imaginative ways. They are very likely to be 'special', so RE teachers are worth consulting on the handling and use of particular objects. The story of Judah Maccabee (Judas Maccabaeus) is a valuable lesson in how to fail to respect objects.

Making resource banks

Almost all the work in this Chapter, on texts, pictures, ICT, and artefacts, aiming to encourage the effective use of resources, has implications for storage. A history department having a large resources centre can transform the work of teachers and pupils alike. There is often a tension, even in the best resourced departments, between secure and orderly storage, and easy use. Pupils are rarely allowed free access to resources, and new teachers in some schools may not be trusted with a key to the resource room. Developing resource banks can therefore take teachers into difficult territory.

Activity

1. Audit the use of resources. This can be a simple survey of pupils, asking them to describe which resources they have used, and how often. Do remember to cover the whole variety of resources available, related to the topics taught, including ICT programmes, handouts, artefacts, libraries, and so on.

2. If you have your own teaching room, go as far as you can towards making it a resources bank for pupils. Start with displays, making sure that the material on the walls is informative and useful for pupils, and include if possible relatively freely available key texts and handouts. In a department where most resources are locked away, the art is to develop cheap resources for your classroom. Hence the following activity.

What are key texts for a history classroom? Certainly dictionaries, encyclopaedias, and chronicles or timelines, are essential.

Topics and trips		
Topic	Possible trips, and the broad aims for each trip	Other departments that might be interested, and why
1		
2		
3		
4		
5		
6		
7		
8		
9		
10		

Figure 5.3   Topics and trips

3.   Plan for each class to collect and produce resources for themselves and other classes. Pupils seem to learn most when they are explaining what they know to other pupils. It is therefore always useful to get them to produce guides to topics, and these guides, if carefully filed, can be just as valuable as commercially-produced materials or those of other teachers. Producing or collecting resources is also an interesting homework task.

When developing resources banks in a school, whether in a single classroom or for a whole department, teachers should aim to pool knowledge and experience, of themselves and pupils, rather than (just) complain about the lack of resources available to them. Teachers of subjects other than history, librarians, and families of pupils, are all likely, if asked, to have resources they would like to contribute. The field is widened further when ICT links are made. A delight of the Open University PGCE programme is the electronic conferencing system. This allows trainee teachers, and now NQTs (called 'alumni'), around the country, to ask for and to donate 'a good worksheet on slavery' or 'a selection of Wilfred Owen's poetry' or whatever.

There are commercially-produced guides to getting free resources, and useful resources are often available from government departments, international agencies, charities, companies, etc. Local libraries are likely to have resources and guides to further resources.

6

Assessment

Aims

The aims of this Chapter are to:

- *help beginning teachers clarify the purposes of assessment;*

- *improve understanding of levels of attainment in history;*

- *improve the techniques of talking and writing about pupil achievements, and about beginning teachers' own achievements.*

Why assess?

"You don't fatten a pig by weighing it"

(Chinese proverb)

Although assessment may be seen as finding out about pupils' knowledge or understanding, it must also have other justifications. Why, after all, do we need to find out about pupils' knowledge, understanding, or whatever? One key purpose of assessment, underplayed by many teachers, is to help pupils learn. '**Formative assessment**' is a phrase recognised by most teachers, yet assessment is too rarely actually used to help pupils learn, perhaps because it is assumed that assessment is 'naturally' formative. Yet, as the saying goes, you don't fatten a pig (simply) by weighing it.

Activity

1. Complete the table in **Figure 6.1**. It is vital that the 'why' column is filled in with more interesting information than "because I would like to know" or "because the department or school would like to know". The 'why' and 'how' columns could include work on 'ipsative' assessment – ie how pupils have improved or worsened compared with their own previous performance.

The previous activity aimed to help you appreciate the value of formative assessment, but **summative assessment** is still likely to worry new teachers. Summative assessment may seem threatening (with test and exam results easily compared between teachers or departments or schools) and can certainly be time-consuming when it comes to report-writing or NRAs. Again, as with formative assessment, it is as important to be clear about the possible purposes of summative assessment as it is to develop techniques (described in later sections of this Chapter) for conducting it.

Activity

1. Fill in the table in **Figure 6.2**. The 'why' column must be sensitive to different possible audiences: teachers are often most concerned with 'value added' measures (ie how much better their pupils did as a result of their teaching), whereas pupils, families, and in recent years governments are often more concerned with 'raw data' (ie how well, in an absolute sense, pupils are performing). The 'how' columns can include statistical analyses. For teachers, one of the most helpful forms of analysis of public exam results is a comparison of history results of pupils with the results of those same pupils in other subjects. This is a subtle and reasonably fair way of measuring the performance of pupils and teachers, though there are many other ways of making use of exam results.

If, in the NQT year, teachers can gain a good, practical, understanding of the need for and uses of assessment, they will be well ahead of many of their peers, and the long hours of assessing (especially the hours spent marking exercise books) can at least seem worthwhile.

The TES of 11 April 1997 had a letter from Phil Taylor: "Chief inspector Chris Woodhead says, in relation to discrepancies between primary schools' performance in the recently-published tables and their inspection reports, "Either OfSTED is rubbish or performance tables are rubbish" (TES, March 28). There is a third possibility."

The need for and uses of formative assessment

National Curriculum and other aspects of history assessment	How is information on this aspect collected?	Why might information on this aspect be useful in 'forming' pupils?	How is assessment information actually used by me in the classroom?	How else could the information be used?
Chronology				
Range and depth of historical knowledge and understanding				
Interpretations of history				
Historical enquiry				
Organisation and communication				
Other aspects of assessment in history				

Figure 6.1 The need for and uses of formative assessment

The need for and uses of summative assessment

Summative assessment processes in history	Why might this summative information be useful?	How is assessment information actually used by me?	How else could the information be used?
End of topic (or term, or year) tests			
Reports, including regular reports to families, and NRAs			
Formal exam results at 16 (mostly GCSEs)			
Formal exam results at 18 (mostly A & AS Levels)			
Other summative assessment processes in history			

Figure 6.2 The need for and uses of summative assessment

Understanding levels and understanding progress

The job of a teacher is to help pupils move on: teachers should not be judged by how able their pupils are, but how much *more* able (or informed, logical, thoughtful, etc) they are as a result of being taught. A common misconception of teachers, when being inspected, is that inspectors are simply judging the abilities of their pupils. Teachers may 'prime' their pupils, with the unfortunate consequence that the observed lessons appear to show no learning: the pupils already know all they need to know. Beginning teachers should of course celebrate the abilities of their pupils, but they must also be comfortable with the fact that pupils are not all exceptionally able and informed. When lessons are being observed, it is entirely proper that pupils should demonstrate a lack of understanding and knowledge: otherwise, why employ a teacher? The art is to *overcome* the 'lack'.

There have also been publications of examples of pupils' work assessed, first by the School Examinations and Assessment Council in 1993.

The *progress* of pupils is the only excuse for teaching, and, in order to understand the progress of pupils, teachers must have an idea of the levels at which pupils are working. Obvious sources of level descriptors are the National Curriculum (NC) attainment target for history and GCSE examination board grade descriptors. New teachers must familiarise themselves with these level descriptors, and often have to overcome fears that there are arcane, mysterious, aspects to the relevant documents.

Activity

Remember that descriptions of achievements at particular levels should always be positive. Level 3 work must be described in terms of the skills and knowledge demonstrated, not the lack of higher level skills or knowledge.

1. Fill in the table in **Figure 6.3**. NQTs may be working with local authority guidance or textbooks that have their own simplified level descriptors. However, it is better, if possible, to produce your own desciptions, as these are likely to be adapted to the needs of your own pupils. Certainly, every teacher should be able to explain why a piece of work by a pupil is considered to be at a particular level, and how it could be done at a higher level.

2. From the work of your own pupils, collect and copy nine pieces of work – three examples of work at each of three consecutive levels. Doing this collection is itself valuable, but, once done, it can also be used to 'moderate' your assessment with your colleagues. Ask colleagues – in your own department or, if necessary, at other schools – whether they agree with your assessments (in terms of levels). Once agreement has been reached, go on to the next activity.

3. Do a similar moderation exercise with pupils. Pupils may be reluctant to 'donate' their own work to be moderated (although this would be better, and may be found acceptable early in a course), in which case, you may be able to use work of pupils in other groups, with names hidden. This illuminates the first of these activities. When you are confident that pupils understand level descriptions, and can apply them to work done, assessment is much easier and less likely to be an area of argument.

History teachers who think it unreasonable to be expected to learn about 'other' subjects should consider their primary colleagues. Most primary teachers are expected to be familiar with National Curriculum assessment patterns in at least ten subjects.

However clear an understanding new teachers have of levels of attainment in history, there are other levels to be considered. All teachers are expected to be teachers of communication skills, numeracy, spirituality, and many other cross-curriculuar issues (addressed in the following Chapter). Beginning teachers should be well-informed on those issues. The English attainment targets are particularly useful for history teachers.

Activity

SCAA have produced a leaflet (History and the use of language) describing various ways in which history teachers can promote language development.

1. Read as much as you can of the English National Curriculum, including the level descriptors. If possible, find or even write a simplified version of these, as already done for history.

2. Ask colleagues in the English department if you can see examples of the work of pupils to whom you teach history. Compare the pupils' work in history and English. Once you are reasonably confident that you can grasp the (approximate) equivalence between levels in the two subjects, you can go on to the next activity.

Levels and grades in history: descriptions for pupils	
NC Level	Description clear to pupils working at that level
1	
2	
3	
4	
5	
6	
7	
8	
Exceptional performance	
GCSE grade	
U	
G	
F	
E	
D	
C	
B	
A	
A*	

Figure 6.3 Levels and grades in history

It is worth pointing out that English teachers could benefit from reading about history teaching. The CHATA Project "*Concepts of History and Teaching Approaches*", described in various as yet unpublished conference papers, and mentioned in works such as Brown (1995), analyses the ways in which pupils develop their ways of expressing themselves in history. For example, they study the uses and meanings of 'and', and 'so' and 'and then' in historical writing.

3. Pick three pupils, and ask them (and their tutors, heads of year, etc) if you can look at their work in every subject. Although a very simple activity, seeing the variety of work done by pupils consistently astonishes teachers. Astonishment is to be cultivated, as predictability tends to lead to self-fulfilling prophecies.

There is a series of books designed for primary schools, and valuable for secondary schools, describing methods of recording significant achievements (eg Glauert, 1996 on science, and Sainsbury, 1996, on English).

The activities described above fit in with movements in schools towards recording significant achievements of pupils, rather than trying to record 'levels' for every little piece of work. It is still important to understand, however, that every lesson should aim to help every pupil learn, and learning can only mean an increase in the level of work done.

Many teachers who compare work by the same pupil in different subjects are surprised that pupils often demonstrate very different levels of skill, understanding or knowledge in the two subjects. Perhaps pupils 'ring-fence' their skills, and use them more sparingly in one subject than in another.

Making a mark: short term assessment

New teachers are rarely prepared for the amount of marking they are expected to do, however often they have been told about the stresses of the job. *Developing as a Teacher of History* must include strategies for coping with the pressure of marking, although, sadly, there is no easy 'solution', and the most experienced teachers are still likely to find marking a time-consuming burden. As was said early in Chapter 3, you can get a reputation for working harder than others, by working the same number of hours as your colleagues, but doing the work before rather than after deadlines. This principle is most valuably put into practice in marking pupils' work. However long you decide to spend on marking, spend it soon. If a set of books takes 90 minutes to mark, spend 90 minutes the day you get the books in, and give the books back in the following lesson. Do not take the books in, keep them for a week or more, then spend 90 minutes marking them: by the time the pupils get the marks, they will care very little about your comments, and will be less likely to be able to respond to your guidance.

The work of a pupil and the comments and marks of a teacher are a kind of conversation, and, like other conversations, the speed of response is what makes the conversation flow. This can be illustrated by considering CB radio. Each person must talk for a time, before switching over to allow the other person to talk. There are no spontaneous 'background' comments (like "hmm" and "oh?") to smooth the conversation, and this lack of immediate response gives the conversation a strangely stilted style. Delaying marking pupils' books makes the teacher-pupil conversation similarly stilted.

Activity

1. Work out how long it takes to complete all the marking you need to do in a week, in order to keep up with departmental or whole-school policies and practices.

2. Use this figure as a basis for working out what a reasonable amount of time would be for you to spend marking, bearing in mind your other commitments (described for the time management exercise in Chapter 3, above).

3. Create a marking schedule: decide when (ie which days of the week and at what times) you need to mark work. The timings should be arranged so that pupils can get their books back in the lesson following the one when they handed their books in. (It may also help to build in a period for 'unexpected' marking, including the marking of books handed in late.) Some teachers may even put their marking schedule up on the classroom wall, so that pupils understand why their books must be given in on a certain day, and why their teacher always looks so tired.

Marking is the most time-consuming form of short-term assessment, so it is worth considering other forms that take less time. The first of these is peer marking. Pupils can learn as much about a topic or skill by assessing their peers as they can by doing the exercise to be assessed. Supportive classes are needed, so that pupils do not see peer marking as a basis for bullying, but if teachers treat peer marking seriously enough, classes will tend to become suitably supportive.

Activity

1. Choose an exercise that illustrates an important aspect of assessment in history (highlighted by the work on **Figure 6.1**, above), that could be peer marked. Arrange for the work to be marked in this way, but 'moderated' by you. Once the moderation has been done, explain to the pupils what the exercise and marking told you about their skills.

A second 'fast' form of short-term assessment is done whilst 'touring' around the class. Sometimes it is more important to check work – ie see that it has been done, and how well structured it is – rather than assess it in a deeper way. For example, on a day homework is to be handed in, it is vital to check that pupils have completed it, so that those who have troubled themselves to do the work feel it was worthwhile, and everyone knows that people who did not complete the work will be 'dealt with'. This can be done by touring the room, while the pupils complete another task, asking to see each pupil's homework.

See also Chapter 4, above, on homework.

Activity

1. Review your lesson plans for the days on which homework is handed in. Ensure that they incorporate 'touring' time, during which you can check on homework and deal appropriately with those who have not completed it.

New teachers who get to grips with the stress of marking perhaps scores or hundreds of books a week should be congratulated. Yet that cannot be the end of the story. If marking is a conversation, then the content of the conversation is as important as the fact that it is carried on. Comments written by teachers should help pupils understand what they have done (right or wrong) and what they should do in the future. Many pupils study history for years getting comments exclusively of the form 'good', 'more needed', 'untidy', or 'unfinished'. Getting a series of 'good' 'good' 'good' 'unfinished' 'good' 'good' 'very good', is unlikely to be very helpful to a pupil. Comments should be varied enough to suggest the teacher has thought about the work, and constructive enough to guide the pupil to being a better historian.

Activity

1. Do a survey of history exercise books, writing down all the stock words and phrases used by you or other markers. Use this list to complete the first column of **Figure 6.4**, below.

2. Fill in the synonyms in the second column. Although this may seem a trivial task, pupils respond very positively to imaginative use of language by markers.

3. Look back at the table on formative assessment (**Figure 6.1**), and choose or invent short phrases (up to seven words) to guide pupils to improvement in each of the categories. Fill in the table in **Figure 6.5**. For example, on 'chronology' you might choose 'good sense of change over time', 'what *era* did this happen in?', or 'clearer if put in date order'. It may be that these phrases are simply shorter versions of the descriptions you used in the exercise in **Figure 6.1**, but rehearsing quick guiding phrases is still a useful task.

Deary (1996b) is all about words, and pupils will surely enjoy the idea of teachers marking their work with 'historical' compliments, and perhaps even historical insults.

Going public: long term assessment and reporting

Long term assessment should be derived from short term assessment. However obvious that may seem, many teachers see them as quite different types of activity, with little bearing on each other. In addition, many reports to parents have almost no connection to the comments made in books. In fact, many reports show little evidence of the subject being reported on, and

The stock market	
Stock word or phrase	**Synonyms**
Excellent	
Good	
Satisfactory (or quite good)	
Needs much improvement	
Unfinished	
Others (from the survey done for the activity above, p 69):	

Figure 6.4   Stock words and phrases, and their synonyms

Guiding phrases for pupils' work	
Quality looked for	Guiding phrases to put in pupils' books
Chronology	
Range and depth of historical knowledge and understanding	
Interpretations of history	
Historical enquiry	
Organisation and communication	
Other aspects of assessment in history	

Figure 6.5   Guiding phrases to put on pupils' books

refer to very general qualities and targets, such as the possibility of trying harder, or the need to concentrate more. New teachers, under pressure throughout the year, can easily forget about longer term issues, yet if they do, they will create more work for themselves when it comes to report-writing (or 'profiling') time.

Schools may use mark books, files, or computer spreadsheets. The term 'mark book' here could refer to any version. It is worth pointing out that as portable computers become cheaper and more popular, registers and mark books are increasingly likely to be kept on spreadsheets. NQTs may wish to pilot such work, if they are confident in the use of computers, and if they have access to one. Perhaps your confidence could persuade the school to provide you with the equipment?

Teachers who have worked to make short term assessment meaningful, should find it relatively easy to complete reports and profiles. The most important connection between the short and the long term is the mark book. A useful mark book will provide reliable information on the work completed by each pupil, and it will also indicate what skills or other qualities have been demonstrated through the year by each pupil. This need not require a huge number of complicated symbols, as long as the teacher knows the purpose of each exercise. For example, if the 'Slavery!' exercise was marked according to pupils' abilities to present contrasting viewpoints on the slave trade, then a simple mark (A, B, C or a number from 1 to 10, or whatever) will indicate each pupil's ability to present viewpoints.

Activity

1. Ask, very politely, to see the mark books of as many teachers as you can, including teachers of subjects other than history. A well-kept mark book is impressive even on first glance. From the mark books you see, review them in two ways. First, look for any technical ideas that may help you. For example, simple things like:

   - pre-printed class lists;
   - a code for lateness;
   - room for comments on pupils;
   - separating or combining registers and marks, etc.

   Second, look to see if, from the mark book alone, you could describe each pupil's subject-specific understanding and skills. If you are unable to see evidence of understanding/skills, this may be because you have not understood the teacher's codes or the meaning of the exercises marked (in which case, ask the teacher what the meanings are), or it may be because the mark book is not fulfilling one of its most important functions. (Perhaps this information is held elsewhere by the teacher.)

2. Use the previous exercise to review your own use of the mark book, paying special attention to its ability to provide you with sufficient information from which to produce reports or profiles.

Having prepared the ground for report-writing, by keeping a useful mark book throughout the year, you are ready to consider report-writing itself. There are many ways to make this activity slightly less of a burden. The first exercise below, involving statement banks, is one way of improving the situation, and is useful whatever system of reporting the school uses. However, some teachers find using statement banks too 'uniform', and they will need other strategies. A looser system, then, is offered in the second exercise. This makes use of the 'writing frame' strategy mentioned above (see page 50), and such writing frames, often unacknowledged, are frequently used by schools in the guidance given to staff on report-writing.

All reports, however produced, are public documents, and this should affect how they are written. There is an entirely appropriate expectation that there be no spelling or grammatical errors on reports, so word-processing reports is advantageous both because word-processors have spelling and grammar checkers, and because a mistake can easily be corrected and the report reprinted. There is also an expectation, in nearly all schools, that reports should be positive rather than negative, and set targets rather than give criticism. The temptation, for teachers of weaker pupils, is to write bland reports as a way of avoiding being negative. However, such bland reports are virtually worthless. Managing to say positive yet realistic things about weaker pupils, and setting clear realistic targets for them, is both the greatest challenge in report-writing, and the one with the greatest rewards. Pupils are particularly appreciative of such reports, and will thank you: they will never thank you for the bland or the dishonest – even the dishonestly complimentary.

As said above (on p 8) targets can be thought of as expressions of hope. Criticisms are always likely to be interpreted as expressions of lack of hope.

Activity

1. Complete the statement banks exercise in **Figure 6.6** below, for one of your classes. If the exercise works well for you, then you may want to do the exercise for every class. Although this will take some time, it will save a considerable amount of time in the longer term. If the exercise is genuinely useful, it should also be useful for departmental colleagues, and it would therefore be sensible to ask members of the department to divide the work up, with each one providing draft statement banks for one year group. The one proviso on the use of statement banks is that teachers using them must adapt the statements to suit their own style (ie their way of writing and dealing with the subject and pupils studying it, and the way the unit of work was actually taught that year), and that they must adapt the statements very carefully to suit each pupil. There will always be a pupil for whom no statement bank could expect to provide appropriate descriptions, and teachers must always be prepared to write distinctive reports in such circumstances.

A teacher who objects to the use of statement banks may wish to skip this exercise and go straight on to the next one. However, there are many teachers who claim a principled objection to statement banks yet whose 'individual' reports are bland, repetitive and of little worth. It would be useful, then, to at least try the statement bank exercise.

2. Complete the writing frame exercise below (**Figure 6.7**). Again, as in the previous exercise, if this is useful, it could be done across the department.

3. Once you have completed a set of reports, or perhaps a few sets, try giving draft versions of them to the pupils, before handing them in. Ask the pupils what they would add or take away from the reports. If you agree with their editing, then of course you can integrate it into the final version; if you disagree, the disagreement should prove a useful basis for genuine negotiation between you.

If you are prepared to commit to statement banks, then this exercise may seem redundant. However, it may still be usefully tried out with pupils: seeing their views on what sort of things should go into a report is most revealing. (See also the following section, on self-assessment.)

Self-assessment: from pupils to teachers

A theme running through this whole Chapter is making assessment clear to pupils. To engage pupils, to help them take control of their own learning, they must be given full opportunities to assess themselves. For this to happen, they need to understand the assessment criteria to be used, and they will benefit from peer marking (as described above, p 69). Pupil self-assessment is also valuable at 'reporting' stages (above, on this page). The main block to pupil self-assessment, however, seems to be teachers' attitudes. Teachers may feel that pupils will treat self-assessment exercises as trivial, or as opportunities for pretending to be other than they are. In order to overcome this, several of the exercises above suggest trialling work with pupils, and all of the exercises should help pupils appreciate the seriousness with which you are treating assessment.

As a new teacher, though, you have an added advantage. You are expected to continue learning all through the NQT year, and will have recently finished an intensive training course. Teachers later in their careers will also be learning, of course, but the priority given to such learning has tended to be lower than that given to NQT learning. So NQTs will be able to appreciate some of the needs of pupils, and some of the pressures associated with assessment and self-assessment. The self-assessment procedures must be well set up to have any significance. Completing a piece of research is one approach (suggested in the following paragraph), but NQTs might wish to set up other forms that better suit their styles of work or their needs.

This situation is likely to change. Already, all teachers wishing to become headteachers are expected to complete an assessed course.

At the start of the NQT year, it is worth planning a small-scale piece of research (as suggested above, p 22), to be completed perhaps in the second term. As this Chapter (along with Chapters 4 and 5) is aimed at the second term, reference should be made again to research and development opportunities. Teachers write an enormous amount, as part of their everyday responsibilities – some have estimated a head of department might produce 50 000 words a year – and the point here is not to add to the burden but to focus on an aspect of work that can be used to help you develop further.

Banking for beginners				

Topic: ....

Category of comment	Examples	Version for best pupils	'Good' version	'Weak' version
Introductory statement	I've taught history to 8P for a year now, and X has proved herself (or himself[1]) an able, committed and imaginative student, helping make the class interesting, creative and enjoyable to teach.			
Course description	In 'The Making of the United Kingdom' we covered ..., and in the 'Revolution' topic later in the year we looked at ...			
Attendance and punctuality	His record of attendance needs to improve to make the most of the educational opportunities available, although his punctuality is good.			
Classwork – general	Her class work is sometimes (often) (always) thorough and detailed, having completed N of the 22 pieces of work set, and she/he can contribute usefully to class discussions. She has produced some excellent display work, too, which helps improve the whole learning atmosphere.			
Homework – general (perhaps incorporating coursework for GCSE students)	X has generally done homework, set almost every week, well, especially the research tasks.			
Historical understanding and skills	In 'The Making of the United Kingdom', he has been able to describe complex situations, explain the causes of different events, and, most usefully, has shown himself able to deal with a wide variety of historical sources of information.			

[1] It is worth producing separate 'male' and 'female' versions of any statement bank to be used, to avoid the possibility of leaving the occasional 'her/him' in the final report, which can easily upset pupils.

Figure 6.6   Statement banks

continued ...

Banking for beginners *(continued)*				
Category of comment	Examples	Version for best pupils	'Good' version	'Weak' version
Best work[2]	Of the work I've seen, the best has been on maps and flags of the United Kingdom (Britain in the 16th Century) (childhood and marriage in the 16th Century) (religions) (the Civil War in England) etc.			
Tests, exams and other formal assessments and self-assessments (as appropriate)	In tests and exams, she has shown evidence of some learning, and this side of her learning will I hope be developed more in the future. I hope she will continue thinking about her own progress, through self-assessment forms and by improving work every week.			
Targets	Maintain his current high level of commitment and hard work. Complete all work to the high standard of his best work. Understand the importance of learning, to improve motivation next term. Improve punctuality and attendance. Complete homework consistently every week. Make the most effective use of class time. Stop poor behaviour blocking effective learning. Practise working under exam conditions, to improve marks. Work to improve the presentation of work.			

[2] However strong or weak a pupil is, it is vital that you and the pupil are clear about the best work. This may be, as in the example, a sub-topic, or it may be one of the historical skills.

Figure 6.6 Statement banks (continued)

Framing reports
Introductory statement
I've taught (class) history for (time), and (pupil) has …
Course description
In this year's history topics (…) we have covered …
Attendance and punctuality
(Pupil)'s attendance has been …
Classwork – general
In class, (pupil) has
Homework – general
Homework has been … completed, and …
Historical understanding and skills
(Pupil) has demonstrated … (using categories from Figure 6.1)
Best work
(Pupil)'s best work this year has been …
Tests, exams and other formal assessments and self-assessments
There were … tests and … exam this year, and (pupil) did … in them, showing in particular …
Targets
Next year (term, etc), (pupil) should …

Figure 6.7 Sample writing frame for preparing reports

Activity

1. If you have completed the research recommended in Chapter 1, consider what value there was for you in completing the exercise, and to what use the work was put by the school.

    If you have not completed the research, analyse why. Blocks to learning are numerous, and only by being honest about what blocks your own work can you be expected to appreciate the blocks to learning of your pupils.

2. Make plans, now, to do a longer piece of work. The plans should not only fit in with, but should be an integral part of, your main responsibilities. For example, if assessment and reporting are two areas of professional development you particularly want to work on, you might plan full versions of some of the exercises in this Chapter, as forms of research and development. If classroom 'control' or 'discipline' are of particular concern to you, it is worth considering, for example, researching by video/audio taping a class in different lessons, analysing their responses to different styles of work. Such work should be set up in discussion with your mentor or with peers in the same position as you. Derive the work from your most pressing needs, and it will kill two birds with one stone; treat research as an additional burden and it will kill you.

    Nichol (1995) has a sound guide to action research for history teachers, explaining how it relates to the work of pupils. The first section of Stern (1995) and all of Stern (1997) provide fuller accounts of research in education.

3. Incorporate in your research some explicit self-assessment. This may simply be a reflective passage, about how what you have learned could affect your work, or it may be a more detailed form of self-assessment. As well as incorporating self-assessment into the research, try to incorporate the research as a whole into a larger-scale piece of work. Currently, a large proportion of teachers complete formal advanced diplomas and degrees such as MAs both for career reasons and for personal development. The first year of teaching is a good year to consider, if not to start, such work: the memories of HEI-based learning are likely to be fresh, and the keenness to learn more should still be there.

    There is more work on this suggested in Chapter 8, below.

7

Making history matter

Aims

Chapters 7 and 8 are aimed at the third term of the NQT year and beyond, and therefore are more reflective and cumulative than previous Chapters. The first aim of Chapter 7 builds, in particular, on previous work in Chapters 1 and 2, and the second aim builds on the work of Chapter 4.

The aims of this Chapter are to:

- *investigate ways in which history addresses key cross-curricular issues;*

- *increase awareness of the diversity of learning needs of pupils;*

- *promote more effective development and use of policies in history departments and beyond.*

History and personal, social, moral, spiritual and cultural development

Whatever history is, and whatever the aim of having history as a school subject is, history teaching is expected to promote pupils' personal, social, moral, spiritual and cultural development (hereafter PSMSC). History teachers, confident in many other ways, have often been surprised by simple questions about this often asked by OfSTED inspectors (for example "How does your subject contribute to the spiritual development of your pupils?"). Cross-curricular issues were built in to the National Curriculum, yet are easily ignored in the rush to subject specialism (which was also built in to the National Curriculum).

Children will develop when at school, and teachers should be aware of how they develop, and how teachers can promote such development. History teachers are lucky to be involved in a subject that lends itself to such issues. The guidance provided to schools included a huge range of cross-curricular issues (up to seventeen, depending on how the issues are divided), including PSMSC, the themes such as citizenship, the dimensions such as equal opportunities, and the skills such as communication. A first strategy for a new teacher is therefore to simplify the list: all the cross-curricular issues can be seen as forms of, or ways of promoting, PSMSC. Simplifying even further, the first activity (**Figure 7.1**) asks only for single lessons that might promote each of the five 'development' areas, and examples are given of lessons that might achieve them. Once an NQT's confidence has been built up, it should be possible to complete **Figure 7.2**, which addresses seventeen separate issues.

Tolley et al (1996b) provides good guidance on OfSTED inspections in general. Nichol (1995) addresses general and specialist history issues, including useful 'aspects of teaching' checklists.

Many practitioners, and even more 'educationists', have their own hierarchy of cross-curricular issues. Nichol (1995) sees political education as one of the key issues facing history teachers. Inman & Buck (1995) focus on personal development, though they range more widely than most accounts. Others might prioritise equal opportunities. NQTs could follow any such hierarchy that they or their schools wish to promote. All the issues, however, will need to be addressed, and each 'hierarchy' is likely to be no more than a method of making sense of an immensely complicated reality.

Activity

1. Complete **Figure 7.1** below. Bear in mind that 'development' does not necessarily mean an 'improvement', for the lives of individual pupils or for the histories of countries. Spiritual development may, for example, involve a thought-provoking experience of the possibility of life having a greater significance than mere survival. Such an experience should be seen as valuable and enriching, but whether or not pupils will thereby be 'improved' is a moot point.

2. When the table has been completed, discuss the lessons with your mentor or colleagues in the department. The discussion should help build up your confidence, and the confidence of other participants, in PSMSC as 'everyday' issues.

3. See if, as a group, you can use the combined skills and knowledge of the department to complete **Figure 7.2**, covering seventeen issues. This is not a trivial exercise, but it should be done quite quickly. Implementing equal opportunities (also covered below), for example, cannot be covered in one lesson, so providing a single example of a lesson addressing the issue, as here, is primarily intended to help teachers understand what they mean by the term.

Lessons incorporating personal, social, moral, spiritual and cultural development	
Issue	**Example of history lesson addressing the issue**
Personal	Eg A lesson investigating the possible problems Edward VI might have had, being such a young monarch, might also draw out the pupils' feelings about their own development. Edward VI is a particularly good example, spending Key Stages 3 and 4, as it were, as King.
Social	Eg Work on rights and duties in the feudal system might complement work on rights and duties within a school. Pupils might be involved in developing class or school rules, following such work in history.
Moral	Eg Lessons on changing attitudes to crime and punishment, or to the 'humanity' of American slaves, would be likely to promote moral development.
Spiritual	Eg An example of spiritual development might be a lesson looking at the shock of the new world-views in the Renaissance or during the English Civil War. (Note that 'secular' topics may promote 'spiritual' development.)
Cultural	Eg Cultural development: entertaining and informative work on, for example, a history of food, might address this issue.

Figure 7.1 Lessons in personal, social, moral, spiritual and cultural development

Cross-curricular issues and history		
Issue	**How this has been developed in history teaching this year**	**How this might be further developed in history teaching**
Personal development		
Social development		
Moral development		
Spiritual development		
Cultural development		
Equal opportunities		
Preparation for multicultural society		
Communication skills		
Numeracy		
Study skills		
Problem solving skills		
ICT skills		
Economic & industrial understanding		
Careers education		
Health education		
Citizenship		
Environmental education		

Figure 7.2 Cross-curricular issues and history

History as communication

After working on the previous exercise (**Figure 7.2**), it is worth concentrating on a selection of cross-curricular issues, starting with communication. The choice, here, is relatively arbitrary. For example, the absence of work on ICT in this Chapter simply reflects its place in Chapter 5, above.

Even more trivially, in 1066 And All That, *it is "what you can remember".*

History is, at least trivially, what people have communicated about the past. As John Slater says (in Lee, 1992, p 45), it is a way of "investigating the past and of authenticating statements about it". There is a wide variety of ways of communicating history, both pre-critical history (often communicated through fiction) and critical history. Recent studies of how children learn history (for example the on-going CHATA Project at the London University Institute of Education), have at last started to look at what exactly children mean when they talk or write (about) history. It is upsetting to such historians to hear some primary teachers talk about the need to cut down on history in order to spend more time on 'essentials' like English. English skills are not 'incidentally' developed in history: history is a subject that at its heart develops pupils' abilities to communicate clearly, to understand the validity of what they say, and to construct narratives linking people and events, causes and effects, and so on. Where else in the curriculum are such communication skills developed so systematically? The vital relationship between history and communication is of course continued into secondary schools.

Graphical communication is also subtly developed in history , critically analysing pictures on Greek vases, the Bayeux 'Tapestry', medieval church paintings, or cartoons about the Second World War, etc.

To exploit the history—communication relationship, beginning teachers should ensure that pupils use a wide range of reading, writing, listening, and talking skills, along with a critical use of graphical and other forms of communication. The following activities ask for a review of work done in class, and much of the work is recommended earlier in this book. It is repeated (or pointed to for a second time) here in order to help you appreciate the variety of forms of communication that can be used to teach and learn history.

Activity

1. Look through your schemes of work, and see where there is a clearly set out **reading** exercise. Popular reading exercises, other than the obvious (and useful) 'read the passage and answer the questions', include paired reading (where one pupil reads a passage out loud to another pupil, with the second pupil taking the lead in answering questions), split reading (where different people in the class read different texts and report back on what they have read to the whole class), reading out in class (giving the teacher's voice a rest), representative reading (where a representative of a group, perhaps someone who has done less writing, reads out the product of a piece of group work), and so on.

2. **Listening** exercises are rarer. A simple yet rich exercise is to get pupils to watch a history video (including archive footage with sounds), asking them to write down a list of all the noises they can hear. Work on this can reveal a surprising amount of information, about differences between periods and about how it might feel to live in a particular period. More traditional listening exercises include getting pupils to produce accounts of what has been said (by the teacher, by fellow pupils, or by people on a video), without taking simultaneous notes.

NQTs should be cautious about using the popular teachers' threat: "carry on behaving like that, and I'll send a copy of the tape to your family". Said with confidence, by a teacher well-known to a class, this can be a humorous pseudo-threat; said by an anxious teacher new to a class and school, this can sound like a genuinely unpleasant threat.

3. **Oral work** can be enhanced if it is recorded, either using audio or video tapes. After initial nervousness or exaggerated behaviour, classes quickly manage to treat the recording process as insignificant. (Teachers are often affected by recording more than pupils, perhaps because they worry about being compromised professionally.) Pupils can do useful work analysing tapes of their own (or others') class at work. Is there room for this in your schemes of work? Recording discussion or debates or presentations (as suggested in this activity) is itself a good way of acknowledging the importance of talk. **Talking** is not always bad. However obvious it may be to teachers that saying 'don't talk' only refers to the need to be silent in a particular set of circumstances, pupils get a different message. Pupils tend to think that talking in class is necessarily bad, either involving 'simple' learning or not involving learning at all. The obligation on teachers is to make sure there are opportunities for valued talking. In what other ways have you promoted this?

4. **Picture work** has already been suggested, with the 'stolen picture' exercise suggested on p 50, above, and DARTing with pictures also suggested on p 50. It is likely, with the textbooks commonly in use in current history courses, that pictures will be fully, if not always well, used by teachers. Analyse your own use of pictures, looking particularly for ways in which you have helped your pupils learn about the ways of 'reading' the picture, critically, rather than thinking of pictures as more or less 'real' versions of 'reality'.

Work by academics such as Gunther Kress (eg Kress & van Leeuwen, 1990, 1996) analyses the grammar of pictures in complex ways. Yet such work also has implications for teachers of history and historians working with images.

Communication is an enormously complex issue. Some teachers and pupils may say that pupils "can write" or "cannot draw", but there are so many forms and levels of writing or drawing that few pupils will be so easily categorisable. A close look at the attainment targets for English, and the end-of-Key-Stage descriptors for art, will ensure that history teachers are aware of the variety of ways in which pupils are expected to communicate.

Access to history: equal opportunities and special needs

History can be seen as a little smug when it treats all events as inevitable. The past may be unchangeable (once it is past), but it is healthy to see it as having been uncertain (at the time). To take a recent example, the political changes in central and eastern Europe from 1989 are already being described by some history teachers and professional historians as an 'inevitable' end of communism – or even as a symptom of the inevitable 'End of History'. Yet historians seemed to show no evidence of this immediately before the events.

Pupils – like the rest of us – can find uncertainty exhilarating. Knowing that there are opportunities for the course of events to go in different directions should inform all history teaching. And it should inform teaching as a whole, as pupils, too, are changeable. Education involves change – 'leading out' new knowledge, understanding and skills. (See above, p 37, for a brief discussion of the etymology of 'education'.) Change can be promoted, or it can be prevented. Teaching is about stimulating learning, and minimising the blocks to learning. Equal opportunities in education means each pupil should be given equal stimulus, or should be helped to overcome equal blocks, in their learning. There is a consensus on the position that equal opportunities is not to do with making every pupil produce the same performance, but rather that where there is no evidence of 'innate' superiority/inferiority there should be no difference in performance under similar circumstances.

Fukuyama (1992) is often put in the 'communism had to end' camp. He did at least propose the 'End of History' before the fall of the Berlin Wall. It is easier finding examples of works failing to predict the imminent end of communism. Halliday (1983, 1986) and Calvocoressi (1968, 1987, 1989) are most definitely not 'bad books' because of their lack of foresight: it is precisely a sign of the unpredictability of history that such fine authors should be 'caught out'.

Blocks to learning, and stimuli to learning, can come from within the pupil, from the teacher, from other people (family, peer group or friends, people in the same class, etc), from 'society' (media, political movements, social conditions, etc), and so on. Because the teacher is just one source of stimulus, it may be that the teacher will have to compensate a pupil for a lack of other stimuli. The teacher may even end up being accused of spending too much energy on a minority of pupils – but if this really is compensating for other conditions, it can be justified. For example, if a pupil is ignored by others in the class (or in their family, or in society), the teacher may wish to give them extra attention. This seems reasonable.

NQTs may already be aware of some of the ways they stimulate/block learning themselves – and this is quite easy to control if, and only if, the teachers are reflective (ie think about what they have done) and are prepared to be flexible. For example, they may be aware that they direct questions unequally to boys and girls, or have different expectations of different groups of pupils. Teachers may, however, be unconscious of some other ways they stimulate/block learning. This is particularly likely where the teacher is new to the school and perhaps to the communities served by the school. Teachers new to a school may be accidentally rude (eg simply by pronouncing names wrongly), they may be insensitive (perhaps by asking "What would your parents think of this behaviour?", if the pupil didn't have, or didn't live with, parents), they may talk or look strange or off-putting to the pupils, or they may look or act like someone who is frightening to a pupil (perhaps a parent). For this reason, teachers need to work out strategies to minimise these unconscious effects on pupils. This can be difficult.

Dean (1995) and Nichol (1995) have good accounts of gender and other equal opportunities issues for history teachers.

Activity

1. Make a provisional list of the ways in which you feel you might 'unevenly' stimulate or block learning. This list may be based on your knowledge of likely blocks/stimuli (particularly if

you have some sociological training), or it may be based on a brief look at the work or results of pupils in your class (perhaps compared with the work or results of those same pupils in other classes).

2. Work out a way of doing some small scale research on that list. It may be that you feel you give unequal attention to boys and girls in your class: research might involve taping a lesson, or getting a pupil to record your interactions with pupils.

3. Work with colleagues to develop strategies for minimising the unevenness of your stimuli/ blocks. This is likely to be an issue that goes well beyond your own work, and affects the whole school.

4. Work with colleagues to develop strategies for minimising blocks to learning – uneven or not – so that pupils are achieving at levels closer to their full potential.

An even more difficult problem for teachers new to a school or area is how much they know about other influences on the pupils. It is no good to think that we, as teachers, simply need to 'treat all the pupils the same'. Pupils are not all the same. We may need to try to compensate for potential blocks to learning that are beyond our direct control. Giving equal opportunities may, therefore, mean finding ways of overcoming their individual blocks to learning, or compensating for their individual lack of other stimulus. This gets us on to the usual topics of equal opportunities – ie race, gender, class, disability, sexual orientation, and so on – as blocks and stimuli are unequally distributed amongst members of particular groups. But do not ever think that these 'categories' are all quite distinct, in need of distinct justification – do not be tempted to think that there is a fixed list of blocks to learning. The lists given out by institutions, or enshrined in laws, are simply examples (perhaps very significant issues, or politically sensitive issues) of some of the infinite number of issues brought up by the question "how do we ensure equal opportunities in education?"

NQTs should be able, even in their hectic first year of teaching, to think about ways of promoting more equal opportunities beyond the classroom. There is considerable value, here as in so many areas of professional development, in systematic research. Simple tasks like recording the number of interactions, suggested above when looking at your own stimuli/ blocks, can provide rich data that can be used to improve your practice and the practice of your colleagues. The research can also be used to tackle 'external' blocks and stimuli. A simple question of facilities available to support children's homework, has in recent years stimulated much political and academic interest. Research on ethnicity, on achievement of girls and boys, and on so many other issues, has helped teachers put their work in context, and has provided clues as to how equal opportunities may be better promoted.

Activity

1. Read at least one book or article describing research on (un)equal opportunities. It should be on a topic relevant to your work in your school. Texts may be found in most HEI libraries, in school staff libraries, in larger or specialist bookshops, on the Internet, and perhaps on your own bookshelves, following your course of initial teacher training. Perhaps now is the time to read something recommended by your tutor?

2. Write a summary of the text (up to one side of an A4 sheet of paper), explaining how it might apply to pupils at your school. If possible, present this summary to your department, or to a working group in the school, for discussion.

If the issues relating to equal opportunities concern blocks and stimuli, then 'special needs' are inevitably closely related. That is the logic of putting them under the same subheading here. Special Educational Needs (in the legal sense) includes pupils who are 'behind' (in some sense) their peers with their learning, unless the lag is a result of having English as a second or subsequent language. A bilingual pupil, with difficulties, should be treated differently (and has another source of extra funding for their education – usually called 'Section 11' funding) to a pupil with other learning difficulties. Of course, the actual help given to bilingual pupils and pupils with SEN could often be very similar. For example, it might be appropriate to give work

Indeed, it is necessary to get away from thinking simply about blocks, but rather, about the enormously rich diversity of interests, skills and knowledge that pupils bring into our classrooms, and how this resource can best be used, as recommended in DfEE 1998c.

It is also worth thinking about how to extend these issues beyond the classroom. As well as making a 'fairer' classroom, can you and the pupils help make a 'fairer' school or community? A book like Macdonald et al (1989), an account of the events leading up to and following the murder of a pupil, can help any teacher appreciate the necessity of addressing issues before they become 'Issues'. That particular book should also be of especial interest to history teachers, as it uses a wide range of research techniques, including imaginative reconstructions.

that is very structured, and which does not include only long pieces of extended writing, to some pupils in both categories.

Some schools use the phrase Special Needs (without the Educational). This is sometimes a slip of the pen, sometimes a way of grouping together SEN and bilingual support, and sometimes a way of including 'gifted' children. 'Gifted' children (yes, I know, all children are gifted, but …) are those who are significantly ahead of (in some sense) their peers. Sometimes the phrase used is 'pupils of marked ability'. Very able pupils may have special needs – ie they may need an adapted curriculum to bring out their best efforts. Schools may therefore have a department of Special Needs catering for three (or even more) groups – pupils with SEN, bilingual pupils, and gifted pupils.

Activity

1. Do a review of how the different learning and language needs of pupils in your school are addressed. This will be a review of:

   - institutional issues (for example, is there a separate department of special needs?);

   - practice (for example, how much support is given in-class, how much out of class?).

It is important to point out that good, exciting, relevant, well resourced, differentiated lessons will almost inevitably be supportive for pupils with SEN, and for bilingual and gifted children. Such teaching will also be more likely to provide more equal opportunities, too. There are not four ways in which you should teach well (one way for each 'special' category, and one way for 'the rest'), but one way.

Avoid the temptation to think, when planning a lesson, that you should first plan for 'the rest', then add an extra/alternative worksheet for each 'special' pupil. This would be appalling, both in terms of your work-load and in terms of the labelling of the 'special' pupils. Your extra work would also often be rejected by its recipients ("why do I have to do this?") or demanded by the others ("why can't we do that sheet?").

Activity

1. There are easier and harder ways of addressing special needs. Find an example, from your own practice or that of colleagues, of an 'easy' and a 'hard' way of teaching that achieves this.

2. Discuss with your mentor or colleagues how the 'harder' way might be made easier. For example, it is difficult to provide 'differentiated' worksheets for individual pupils. Could there be a pooling of such sheets (if they are needed), or could the principles used to produce them be applied to the 'mainstream' worksheets?

3. Discuss with your mentor or colleagues how the 'easier' way might be applied in more circumstances in the department. For example, a good oral exercise might be discussed in a department meeting; differentiated homework tasks might be planned at the start of the year and reviewed later in the year.

Equal opportunities and special needs are issues for a lifetime. Both require teachers to be sensitive and constantly reviewing their own work. History teachers, in particular, may find it rewarding to look at these issues *with* their pupils: there are many ways in which opportunities and expectations change over time. Pupils find it fascinating tackling change, and how their own lives would have been affected by being lived at different times. By looking at the issues in this way, teachers are making history matter more, and are highlighting vital educational topics at the same time.

History and policy in department and school

One thing that all the cross-curricular issues covered in this Chapter hold in common, is that they are affected enormously by the nature and implementation of whole-school and departmental policies. The Chapter should therefore end by looking at 'policy' in general. Towards the end of the NQT year, in any case, is a good time to look at policy, with a clearer understanding of how policy is or could be implemented.

Many policies, especially those developed and implemented by school leaders and managers,

The White Paper Excellence in Schools *(DfEE, 1997) addresses both homework and policy, proposing consultation on "what form should the homework guidelines take, and how can they be made most effective in practice?". DfEE (1988b) continues this debate.*

come up against problems of perspective. From the manager's point of view, the whole school is generally seen as benefitting from consistency, with consistency being maintained by creating and monitoring policies. Teachers, on the other hand, tend to see whole-school consistency as reducing the importance of individual professional judgement, and as weakening the influence of departments. This is a common problem with whole-school homework policies. The more specific the policy is (eg 'set homework once a week'), the more individual teachers and departments will protest, either by trying to change the policy as it is being made, or, more commonly, by ignoring the policy once it has been passed. The more vague or general the policy is (eg 'homework is a good thing'), the less able it is to have any effect. One strategy for avoiding these problems is to concentrate on helping your department to develop its own policies, making them distinctly 'historical'.

Activity

1. Choose an issue, and find out about the whole school, department, and your (actual) policy – this last might equally be called your *practice*. The issue should be one of those covered elsewhere in this Chapter. Look for similarities and differences between policies at different 'levels', and in practice. Build on similarities; use differences as a source of change and development.

Jones & Sparks (1996) is helpful on the relationship between members of a department.

2. Ask your subject leader or head of department if you can help draft a departmental policy on an issue. After they have been picked up off the floor (it being such a surprise to be offered such work), explain that it is useful to be fully involved, and that your ideas, though based on less experience, may yet be stimulating and effective. The HoD would be mean not to allow you to do some such work.

8

Professional development in history

Aims

The aims of this Chapter are to:

- *help beginning teachers take charge of their own professional development (building on Chapters 1 and 4, above) and in so doing, further their progress towards acquiring 'advanced skills' status as a teacher, or appointment as a subject leader;*

- *promote an understanding of school hierarchies, management, and leadership (including subject leadership), in order to help new teachers understand their own possible careers;*

- *clarify sources of further professional development available.*

What is expertise in history teaching?

This Chapter looks again at being an 'expert' (or 'advanced skills teacher') in the classroom, and, beyond that, to the possibility of continuing improvement. In Chapter 1, it was pointed out that a proper measure of teachers' competence was pupils' learning. The 'standards' work in that Chapter also included a target-setting exercise (p 8). Chapter 4 included work on achievements and on expertise (p 38–40, and **Figure 4.2**). A principle common to both Chapters 1 and 4 is that if a teacher is to claim expertise, the expertise should be seen to be helpful for pupils. The present Chapter, therefore, looks again at expertise and at pupil learning, and assumes that the previous activities have been completed. (If the previous activities were missed out, it is recommended that they be done now.)

The first set of activities asks beginning teachers to describe aspects of their own expertise. Teachers are notoriously reluctant to sing their own praises, so it is hoped that you will not avoid the activities out of modesty. To be able to teach at all is impressive. The idea that a group of 30 adolescents be forced to stay in a room, day after day, to study subjects they may have no interest in, is bizarre in itself. Parents may struggle to get a single adolescent child to wake up, or to say "hello", or (on food, entertainment, holidays, etc) to reach a level of enthusiasm as high as indifference. Yet those same parents expect teachers to have wonderful lessons with groups of dozens of the same adolescents. And, remarkably, teachers expect the same. When a few lessons are less than thrilling, teachers tend to think they are completely useless. Surely not. Be joyful that some lessons work well, and try to make sure the rest are professionally handled and provide opportunities for learning by all. The activities below, then, should be completed in the spirit of pleasant surprise that you have proven yourself genuinely 'expert' some of the time, even in your first years of teaching.

Activity

1. One model of 'expertise' (briefly described on p 27–28 and p 40, above) is that of the **breadth of your professional knowledge**.

   - On a single piece of A4 paper, draw a map of the history topics you teach, covering the whole page.

   - Using coloured pencils or other shading patterns (ask a geography teacher if you want to know more techniques) shade the map in. One colour should be for those areas you felt expert in at the start of the teaching year, a second colour for those (extra) areas you felt expert in half way through the year, and a third colour for the areas you now feel expert in. The three colours will form 'expanding circles'.

   History teachers should find teaching a topic, even one they have studied at university, makes them feel considerably more expert. They may, of course, realise gaps in their knowledge, as a result of awkward questions asked by pupils, but, over time, they almost always increase their expertise

2. Do the same exercise for **teaching techniques**. That is, draw all the techniques known to humankind, and shade in those you feel you have been expert in (at some time during the year). The appropriate measure of expertise here, as elsewhere, is that pupils have

Roland Barth (1990) suggests that any school leader should ask the question of any policy or practice in the school, "how does it help learning?" Barth is referring to learning by all in the school. However, it is pupil learning that many groups, including parents, are likely to see as most significant.

Appraisal, a system intended to record the achievements of teachers, is seen by many as a way of finding faults.

If one aspect of your work, in each year of your teaching career, is excellent, then you will have achieved more than many workers.

See Tolley et al (1996f) introductory section and pages 35ff, and pages 25ff, on continually developing professional competence.

There is no simple, objective, measure of subject knowledge. Institutions often use 'studied at first degree level' as evidence for subject knowledge in a particular area. Yet there must be other ways of attaining subject knowledge. A rule of thumb could be that subject knowledge is sufficiently high, within a topic, for you to be able to understand and incorporate new information. Not 'completeness', then, but enough understanding to be able to cope with 'the rest'.

benefitted from your teaching. Perhaps you could write a list of all the teaching techniques you have used with a group of pupils, and ask them which most helped them learn.

3. Another way of looking at expertise is to think of the **depth of your understanding or knowledge**. What would your specialist topic be on an historical *Mastermind*? Which lesson would you expect pupils to remember (for good reasons) once they were adults? Make a list of those subject topics, or teaching techniques, that you believe are your 'expert' topics within the school. You should avoid measuring yourself against professional historians, based in universities, or teacher trainers, whose job it is to describe or model particular teaching techniques. Instead, measure yourself, as honestly as you can, against your colleagues in the department and the rest of the school. Are there topics or techniques on which you are or could be treated as an expert?

There are two possible problems with this exercise: the problems of excess arrogance and excess modesty. Sometimes, NQTs dismiss the skills and knowledge of their more senior colleagues, and, with the freshness of the new teacher, treat others as jaded and old-fashioned. They feel that they are the only people who are 'current'. This can give the (correct) impression of arrogance. However, the opposite can also happen, where NQTs can feel in awe of colleagues, thinking they know virtually nothing about history (because colleagues can talk with confidence about all the school's history topics), and absolutely nothing about how to teach (because colleagues seem to cope so well). This exercise is intended to avoid both problems, by focusing on individual areas of 'expertise', thereby avoiding comprehensive arrogance (by specialising) and undue modesty (by picking out something, at least, that is good).

4. Expertise can also be described in terms of **progress**. Fill in the graph in **Figure 8.1**. Here, the emphasis is on changes through the year. For each of the high and low points on your graph, write in what made it a high or low point. This is an exercise that may seem trivial, but it can generate tremendously useful information. The graph drawn, and its annotations, should be discussed with colleagues or mentors: the exercise is most likely to be effective if several people complete their own graphs, and then discuss them, first in pairs, then as a whole group.

An 'expert', in this model, is someone who makes considerable (if interrupted) progress, or who makes consistent progress in all areas, from a sound professional base.

If you keep good enough records of your work, so that each year's work can build on the previous year's work, then you should find the job becoming more satisfying. That is, the 'graph' of each year should have a higher 'base line'.

Teachers want to be expert because that makes the work more satisfying – as pupils are likely to learn more and as the work itself is more fulfilling. As a history teacher, however, it is wise to learn one of history's own lessons: no-one is expert enough to avoid the possibility of failure. When a teacher demonstrates increasing expertise, there should be a warning bell sounded. The pay and promotion prospects, tied in with evidence of expertise, bring with them changes in rôle requiring quite new skills and approaches. That is, the reward for expertise can sometimes be promotion, and promotion often seems to make prior expertise irrelevant.

'The Peter Principle' is that an organisation will promote a worker 'to his level of incompetence'. This deeply cynical principle, however, has its good side: it suggests that promotion is still likely as long as you can do the job. (It also suggests that women are excluded – either from jobs or from the Principle.)

One aim of this and the following section, therefore, is to promote a model of expertise that is transferable to different positions in the teaching profession. Another linked aim is to help new teachers focus on **expertise-and-promotion**. Some NQTs focus on survival alone (equivalent to wishing one's life away), others on survival-and-promotion (a recipe for an unsatisfying if well-paid career), others on survival-and-classroom-expertise (a recipe for a satisfying yet poorly paid career).

The first year in a job is also more likely to be on a temporary contract. If it is, then moving on must be considered. Some NQTs find this situation refreshing – as they have an 'excuse' to leave if they are unhappy.

From managing pupils to managing teachers: careering through history

> "If A is a success in life, then A equals x plus y plus z. Work is x; y is play; and z is keeping your mouth shut"
>
> Albert Einstein

The NQT year is the best year in which to think about promotion within or beyond the school. Managers expect many new teachers to move on quickly, and the knowledge that a teacher is

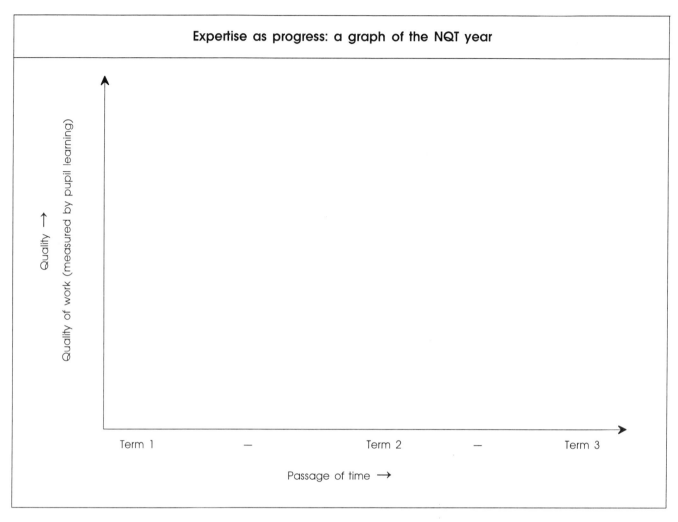

Figure 8.1   Graph of progress through the NQT year

looking elsewhere can focus management minds on making that teacher's work in the school more satisfying. *Thinking* about moving on does not, however, mean that NQTs should assume they *will* move on. It is hard work getting used to any job; changing jobs is even harder. The activities below therefore ask you to consider the work of the head of department or subject leader, and the senior manager (or school leader). Understanding these rôles will help you move on, if that is what you want, and will help you get the most out of people higher in the hierarchy, even if you do not wish to join them.

The present author, when teaching in a school, was visited during tutor time by the Head who, commendably, came to talk to each tutor group. He began talking to them, "Mr Stern has been working for me for two years, and … ". I was thinking "No, I don't work for him; he works for me". It was a time to realise that within hierarchies, people can have different views of their rôles, without necessarily being aware of them. The hierarchy could be in the form (popular in depictions of feudalism) of an upward-pointing triangle, with the 'junior' staff supporting the 'senior' staff; or it could be a downward-pointing triangle, with more senior staff supporting the more junior.

Activity

1. Consider whether, within your school hierarchy of professionals, the 'higher' people work for the 'lower' people, or the 'lower' people work for the 'higher' people. This is as much a matter of attitude as action, so it can be difficult to research. Asking the question (even of oneself) may however be enough to generate an answer.

2. Now, consider how the hierarchy works in your own classroom. Are you, as the teacher, working for the pupils, or are they working for you? Again, the evidence may be difficult to find, but asking the question is still valuable.

3. Having done the previous two activities, you can categorise your situation, using the following three descriptions. The most common situations could be described as:

    • **being pulled apart**: this is the situation in which you feel you are working for the pupils and for the management/leaders; you are constantly trying to please both groups of people, and never feel able to do either well.

Taylor (1996) gives a sympathetic account of Joseph Lancaster's monitorial system.

- **the monitor**: this is the situation where you are working for more senior staff, and have got all the pupils to work for you, as teachers would be expected to do under the monitorial system of the last century.

- **the supportive teacher**: is the situation where you work for the pupils, and are supported in this task by more senior staff.

Marland (1971) was a sound guide to subject leadership, if couched in the older language of the 'head of department'. A more recent book is Jones & Sparks (1996). Brown (1995) looks specifically at managing history.

Given the work done above on your own situation, it is now worth considering what you would do if, or when, you become a head of department (HoD) or subject leader. The scenarios below happen often enough in school. There may well not be an obvious 'right' answer, or easy solution, of course. The advantage of thinking about these issues at every stage of a career, rather than when/if you become a head of department or subject leader, is that you will be better able to seek the most appropriate support from others if you have already worked out what you would do in their shoes. (Some HoDs, when presented with a problem, say "Well, what would you like me to do?")

- *A teacher says "Can we have a pupil excluded?" What would you as HoD need to find out from the teacher and/or from the pupil? How would you decide whether or not to recommend an exclusion? If you are going to recommend one, how would you go about the practical details?*

- *A teacher acts in a way that you think is unprofessional. The teacher says there was a 'rapport' with a pupil, and that it hadn't been a busy day, anyway, so they went off to the shops and bought the pupil some new, trendier, clothes. As HoD, how would you deal with the situation?*

- *A visiting inspector/adviser suggests that there is too little experiential learning in history. What sort of approaches would you recommend to your colleagues to address this problem? (The approaches may include ways of convincing the inspector, on a subsequent visit, that you and your colleagues were misunderstood on the previous visit, and had always been concerned with experiential learning.)*

- *You are asked to address a meeting of parents of prospective GCSE pupils. What would you most want to tell them about GCSE history, and how would you 'research' what you would want to say?*

- *Two teachers have clearly had a disagreement with each other. They both seem quite upset about the row. What can you do as HoD? What are your priorities in this situation? As well as what you could do now, in the school, is there anything you could do later?*

- *A parent telephones you to complain that another teacher in your department is trying to indoctrinate the pupils, including their child. What would you say to the parent, there and then, and, in the longer term, how would you investigate or otherwise deal with the issue?*

- *A teacher has had a distressing time in a class. The teacher would like to know what has happened to the class. You are asked to find out. As HoD, would you want to or be able to find this out? How would you go about this and how too would you deal with the teacher?*

- *Books in your department seem to be going missing at an alarming rate, perhaps because teachers are not keeping track of them. As HoD, how would you investigate and deal with this situation, without creating a huge overload of work for you or other teachers in the department?*

Much as being a history teacher is likely to lead you to defend the unique place of history in the curriculum, a professional wishing to promote a broad and balanced curriculum for the pupils should be able to consider alternatives to 'pure' history courses.

- *It has been suggested (ie you have overheard some 'gossip') that the school may get rid of GCSE history, and introduce a humanities or modular social science course. As HoD, how might you defend the position of GCSE history, and how might you plan to contribute to (or take over) the alternative course?*

- *You have been asked to produce a development plan for your department, based on the school's newly decided 'mission statement', but the members of your department are contemptuous, saying they are too busy teaching to bother with filling in pointless forms for the school's over-promoted management team. How do you, as a middle manager or subject leader, help members of your department to appreciate the advantages (to them, to the department, and to the pupils) of completing the exercise – perhaps even with enthusiasm?*

As a consultant, one of my favourite jobs is going in to a school, reading about the whole school aims and policies, and talking to the teachers in one department about what they do and how they work. A couple of days later, I'll go in with my account of what the teachers have said, related to whole school policies: this takes the form of a set of departmental policies or a departmental development plan. Every time I've done this, so far, the teachers have said something like "this looks really good: do you mean these are what our department's policies should look like?" I generally reply that these are what the department's policies really are, whatever it says in the departmental handbook. One happy department. Like a good therapist, a good consultant simply repeats back to the client what the client tells them, in such a way that the client thinks the consultant has come up with really good advice. In fact, the advice is only good because it is what the client does anyway. (There is still, of course a value in having an 'external audit', simply because an outsider can sometimes see both the wood and the trees, and will have seen woods and trees elsewhere, to put the situation in perspective.)

- *A particularly sophisticated computer has become available in the school, and will be given to the department that comes up with the most convincing reasons for needing a (or another) computer of this kind. Give your reasons for the machine going to the history department.*

- *It is very near the end of the financial year. The school wishes to avoid 'underspends' in the INSET department. Come up with the most imaginative, compelling, description of how the INSET money could be spent in your department.*

Senior managers or school leaders, at the top of the hierarchy, may work with new teachers in various ways. They may provide you with INSET; they may help in supporting your department's policies and practices; and they are very likely to be developing whole-school policies and practices that you are expected to implement.

Activity

1. List the ways in which senior managers or leaders work with you. This audit could be ranked – putting the work in order of its usefulness for you. (If it is ranked, then be aware that the value of the work of senior managers may not be immediately apparent: they are likely to take a long-term view, from a whole-school perspective.)

2. Make a list of all the things that you would *like* senior managers or leaders to do for you (excluding the INSET suggested in the following activity). This list should of course be realistic, and it should also explain how the managers' work might be organised to make this possible. So, for example, if you would like 'more support', what exact support would you like, and what do you think the managers should do less of, or do differently, in order to allow them to support you more?

3. Describe how you could contribute to the senior managers' need for research, through the INSET programme. Senior managers are in general responsible for large scale changes in a school. Change should be based on knowledge and understanding, and this means research. The most obvious basis of research is the school itself, and school managers can do this through the INSET programme. How could your needs and their needs be matched?

Managing yourself: having the confidence to carry on learning, reflecting, and action planning

Expertise has been addressed, along with the rôle of managers and leaders. The intention has been to look at teaching as a whole career. To round off the book, there is a recapitulation of the ways of managing yourself, concentrating on research and reflective practice, and an annotated list of some of the books that might be useful in taking your development further.

Frase (1990 and 1992) are interesting practical books on school management, and Grace (1995) is good on the relationship between management and leadership. Roberts (1989) is a novel way of approaching leadership, even if the book is based on a rather unreliable account of Attila the Hun.

Davies & Ellison (1997) is a good account of current views on school leadership. It may help you to know what leaders are likely to be reading at the moment.

As new teachers, you are in a strong position to influence the whole school's INSET programme, as you have an 'excuse' to require INSET, and, I hope, it is difficult to palm you off with poor quality INSET. Exploit your position.

In Chapter 1 research was first recommended, as a focus for professional development. A 2000 word report, suggested there, could be written in a day, though of course the research leading up to it (which might well be part of your everyday responsibilities) might take longer. Chapter 6 built on this, suggesting that you can analyse the value and use of research, and make the research central to your own clearest needs. By the third term, it is certainly worth considering again the rôle of research in your professional development, as has been done in the last activity above.

This could, as previously suggested, form part of a larger 'Professional Development Portfolio', tied in to progress throughout a career. Bell (1987) is a comprehensive guide to completing education research.

Activity

1. If you have not already done this, then arrange a peer observation exercise. Mutual observation, described in Chapter 4 is a way for all teachers to carry on learning about the job. The more purposive the exercise, the better. As part of a research project, it is almost always possible to create opportunities for other teachers to observe you, and for you to observe others. Research on gender might include systematically observing the activities and interactions of boys and girls in the classroom; research on the uses of sources in history might include observing ways of helping pupils learn from videos in class, and so on.

You may, properly, wish to gain recognition for any research you are involved in, and many new teachers will wish to look at completing MAs, or contributing to public documents by publishing articles in professional journals or (more likely) publishing materials that could be used by other schools.

Activity

1. Discuss with your mentor or colleagues what would be the advantages of completing a further formal qualification and/or getting material published. You may well wish to put this off until you have been teaching for a number of years, yet it is worth considering it early.

See Tolley et al (1996a p 7) and on job enrichment, job swaps, exchanges, etc, see Tolley et al (1996f) Chapter 6.

Another way of reflecting on your abilities and career is to look at alternative careers, related to teaching (such as youth and community work, the inspectorate, educational publishing, etc), or completely unrelated. Whatever your attitude to the teaching profession, it is likely to be clarified if the alternatives are well considered: there is a big difference between finding teaching difficult while thinking it a 'trap', and finding teaching difficult while realising it is the best job for you.

Activity

This is a form of action planning, complemented by the final activity, below. It may be worth looking back over the whole of this book, and the activities completed, in order to gain a realistic view of your progress as a beginning teacher of history. Meanwhile, good luck!

1. Plan an 'escape route' to another career. Many schools have what are called 'escape committees', made up of teachers wishing to leave the school (or wishing to leave teaching altogether). Although such 'committees' may seem rather negative, considering alternatives is a genuine stress-reliever. If alternatives are discovered, they can be seen as 'hopes'; if there are no alternatives (for you), then you may feel better about your original choice of school or career.

2. Choose at least one book you have not previously read, from the bibliography below, and read it. This should be a book you feel will help you develop further. It is, incidentally, worth asking your mentor or the school to buy such books as you feel will be helpful to teachers. Sections of school libraries set aside for teachers have become more common in recent years. Contribute to the use of such facilities. As a history teacher, you surely appreciate the power of books.

Bibliography

Sourcebooks for development: an annotated bibliography

This section includes full bibliographical details of books and most other references mentioned in the text, with further details and comments. The annotations are not, of course, intended to replace the originals. Two further points are worth making. Firstly, no book list can include all the (most important) books for history teachers. There are so many useful books, all a book list can do is recommend one possible book-based route to professional development. Many superb books will be missed off any one published bibliography, and teachers should feel confident to treat their own favourite texts as of continuing value, whether or not the books are on a list. Secondly, there are many places, other than books, for teachers to search. Television, CD-Roms, and the Internet are all rich sources of information and advice, and academic, professional, and popular journals have a huge amount to offer. The main reason for concentrating on books here is that books are generally more easily available (at bookshops, teachers' centres, and libraries, if necessary through the inter-library loans schemes), and have a greater permanence.

New teachers looking for television and video sources should look to resources held in their school or by colleagues in their homes, as so many people collect videos.

CD-Roms are regularly reviewed, in print and on the Internet, by BECTa (the British Educational Communications and Technology Agency) – formerly NCET (the National Council for Educational Technology).

The Internet itself is best searched for short periods, regularly. If you put an enormous effort into finding every useful site, in preparation for a year's teaching, the resulting list of addresses will be well out of date half way through that year.

Journals are most easily accessed in Higher Education libraries, although most history teachers will presumably want a personal subscription to at least one journal like *History Today*.

Barber, M (1996) *The Learning Game: Arguments for an Education Revolution*; London: Gollancz.

An influential book on present and future schooling in the UK.

Barth, R S (1990) *Improving Schools from Within: Teachers, Parents, and Principals Can Make the Difference*; San Francsisco: Jossy-Bass.

Written by the head of Harvard's Principals' Center. Teachers and principals (ie headteachers) are seen as learners, so that the school can become a community of learners.

Battersby, J (1995) *Teaching Geography at Key Stage 3*; Cambridge: Chris Kington.

Companion to Nichol (1995) on history.

Bell, J (1987) *Doing Your Research Project: A Guide for First-Time Researchers in Education and Social Science*; Buckingham: Open University Press.

A comprehensive blow-by-blow account of techniques of education research.

Benn, C, & Chitty, C (1996) *Thirty Years On: Is Comprehensive Education Alive and Well or Struggling to Survive?*; London: Fulton.

New analysis, thirty-one years after the defining moment of 10/65, of comprehensives. A big book, promising much by tackling older issues in the current context.

Benton, M & Benton, P (1990) *Double Vision: Reading Paintings – Reading Poems – Reading Paintings*; London: Hodder & Stoughton.

Superb book of paintings, and poems written about them (or vice versa), and exercises relating to both. Some of the best example of DARTs work.

Blatchford, P & Sharp, S (eds) (1994) *Breaktime and the School: Understanding and Changing Playground Behaviour*; London: Routledge.

Review of research and initiatives on breaktime in primary and secondary schools.

Bourdillon, H (ed) (1994) *Teaching History*; London: Routledge/Open University.

Core text for the Open University's Secondary PGCE in history. Many invaluable articles for students and for new and experienced teachers, covering theory and practice, including the first version of the National Curriculum, and much beyond.

Brown, D (1995–1996 edition, published 1995, etc) *Goldmine: Finding Free and Low-cost Resources for Teaching*; Aldershot: Ashgate.

A catalogue of free or cheap materials for teachers.

Brown, R (1995) *Managing the Learning of History*; London: Fulton.

Brown considers what is special about history, and how to manage the subject. Teaching, like history, is full of uncertainty (multidimensional, simultaneous, immediate, unpredictable, public, and has its own history), but mustn't (in either arena) get overwhelmed by uncertainty.

Brown, S & Race, P (1995) *Assess Your Own Teaching Quality*; London: Kogan Page.

A valuable, simple, approach to self-assessment by teachers.

Burns, R (1982) *Self-Concept Development and Education*; Eastbourne: Holt, Rinehart & Winston.

Heavyweight, American-style (though British), psychological text, but designed for initial teacher training & INSET – and therefore including much practical information.

Calvocoressi, P (1968, 5th edition 1987, fourth impression 1989) *World Politics Since 1945*; London: Longman.

Fine book, written as close as you could get to the 'fall' of communism, yet with no inclination. The 1980s are compared with the 60s and 70s as 'surlier' (p 49), and there is no hint of possible collapse.

Capel, S, Leask, M & Turner, T (1997) *Starting to Teach in the Secondary School: A Companion for the Newly Qualified Teacher*; London: Routledge.

Generic NQT book.

Carrington, B & Troyna, B (eds) (1988) *Children and Controversial Issues: Strategies for the Early and Middle Years of Schooling*; London: Falmer.

Fearful of the effects of the Education Reform Act in squeezing out controversial issues from the curriculum, the book is particularly keen to demonstrate the sophisticated discourse on controversial issues demonstrated by children of all ages. As well as general issues to do with the status and rôle of the teacher, there are chapters on specific issues – the world of work, sexism, race and conflict, sexuality, and racism.

Cartwright, F F (1972) *Disease and History*; London: Hart-Davis, MacGibbon.

An account of various ways in which history may have been affected by disease. For connoisseurs of trivia, though it is a terribly serious topic, of course.

Chambers, J & Hood, M (1992) *Picture the Past: Art Ideas to Recreate History for Children Aged Five to Eleven*; Twickenham: Belair.

A good visual guide.

Claire, H (1996) *Reclaiming Our Pasts: Equality and Diversity in the Primary History Curriculum*; Stoke-on-Trent: Trentham.

A book about history and of history – especially the history of women, non-European, black, or (British) ethnic minority people, the working class and other people 'from below'. Processes like recounting family histories, using stories, and describing famous people, are all carefully described for KS1 and 2 – and all useable at KS3. The book concludes with chapters on 'lives of distinction connected with Britain', resources (books on famous people, children's fiction, and non-fiction and adult resources), and immigration and emigration patterns in Britain.

Clare, J D (1995) *The Twentieth Century: Options in History Programme of Study*; Walton-on-Thames: Nelson.

A teachers' book, to back up pupil textbook. The work on differentiation is particularly good, as is the author's justification for his approach.

Copeland, T (1991) *A Teacher's Guide to Maths and the Historic Environment*; London: English Heritage.

How to do Maths on sites. A good way, too, of getting joint funding for a trip out.

Copeland, T (1993) *A Teacher's Guide to Geography and the Historic Environment*; London: English Heritage.

Particularly useful for combined history – geography field trips, highlighting what elements of the National Curriculum have hidden, that is, the similarities between the subjects.

Croall, J (1992) *Dig for History: Active Learning Across the Curriculum*; Crediton, Devon: Southgate.

The book of the Living Archive Project team working on the Dig Where You Stand scheme. A lively book of cross-curricular projects, mostly from around the edges of the UK, involving history, drama, etc.

Daniels, H (ed) (1996) *An Introduction to Vygotsky*; London: Routledge.

Wide-ranging and refreshing articles about the psychologist who is more often referred to than read.

Davies, B & Ellison, L (1997) *School Leadership for the 21st Century: a Competency and Knowledge Approach*; London: Routledge.

A comprehensive book on the current views on leadership/management. Competence, self-esteem, quality (slightly contrasted to school effectiveness/improvement), the learning organisation, finance, and marketing, are amongst the issues covered.

Dean, J (1995) *Teaching History at Key Stage 2*; Cambridge: Chris Kington.

Chapter 1, on key issues, is very rich. Chapter 2 is on the National Curriculum. Chapter 3 on ICT, including CD-Roms, class databases. There's also a bank of useful materials.

Deary, T (1996a) *Horrible Histories: The Slimy Stuarts*; London: Scholastic.

One of a long list of impressive, and immensely popular horrible history books (The Terrible Tudors, The Awesome Egyptians, The Rotten Romans, The Vile Victorians, The Vicious Vikings, The Blitzed Brits, The Groovy Greeks, Cruel Kings and Mean Queens, Dreadful Diary, etc)

Deary, T (1996b) *Horrible Histories: Wicked Words*; London: Scholastic.

Engaging etymologies.

Department for Education and Employment (DfEE) (1997) *Excellence in Schools*; London: HMSO.

The new Labour government's first White Paper; more green than white, as it is full of ideas for consultation rather than legislative plans. Commendable stresses on early years, and homework. Also looks at 'modernising the comprehensive principle', including making setting the norm in schools, etc.

Department for Education and Employment (DfEE) (1998a) *Teaching: High Status, High Standards: Requirements for Courses of Initial Teacher Training: Circular Number 4/98*; London: Teacher Training Agency.

The national curriculum for ITT. Amongst other interesting bits and pieces, is a definition of ICT as 'e.g. computers, the Internet, CD-ROM and other software, television and radio, video, cameras and other equipment'.

Department for Education and Employment (DfEE) (1998b) *Extending opportunity: a national framework for study support*; London: DfEE.

Good advice and contacts on various forms of supporting study, and some accompanying guidance on homework.

Department for Education and Employment (DfEE) (1998c) *Induction for New Teachers: A Consultation Document*; London: DfEE.

Draft standards for the induction year, requiring continued work on the QTS standards, and adding much more, including, helpfully, the need for new teachers to 'identify and take advantage of the opportunities offered by ethnic and cultural diversity', and to 'take responsibility for their own future professional development and keep up to date with research and developments in pedagogy and in the subject(s) they teach'.

Department of Education and Science (1989) *Discipline in Schools: Report of the Committee of Enquiry chaired by Lord Elton*; London: HMSO.

Report on behaviour in maintained mainstream primary and secondary schools. The committee was set up following press scares about violence against teachers – and what should be done about it. The report really is a model of how to write a powerful and sensitive guide to good practice.

Dickinson, A (ed) (1992) *Perspectives on Change in History Education: A Publication Based on the Proceedings of the Second Anglo-Hungarian History Teaching Seminar*; London: Institute of Education.

A collection of conference papers from many of the leading players in the field. Perhaps the international perspective encouraged the writers to look at broad issues.

Durbin, G, Morris, S, & Wilkinson, S (1990) *A Teacher's Guide to Learning from Objects*; London: English Heritage.

Investigative work, to help pupils really think about artefacts. The book would surely also be useful for teachers of art, RE, and design & technology.

Farmer, A & Knight, P (1995) *Active History in Key Stages 3 and 4*; London: Fulton.

A book of active history. Historical reasoning 'is distinctive and cannot be contained within general learning theories'. Twelve pointers to effective history teaching, including classroom, departmental issues, and good accounts of purposes and concepts. Active history is underpinned by an interest in mental activity, purposeful tasks, varied and therefore motivating, depth studies, using texts as resources to build on. Active history would also help develop most of the qualities most prized by employers, too. Several National Curriculum topics are described, with excellent suggestions of many 'key' tasks.

Ferguson, N (ed) (1997) *Virtual History*; London: Picador.

The book of what-ifs, or counter-factual history, pepped up with chaos theory, postmodernism, subjective narratives, etc.

Fish, D (1995) *Quality Mentoring for Student Teachers: A Principled Approach to Practice*; London: Fulton.

A good guide to mentoring – centred on professionalism, rather than just good classroom practice; education, rather than just training.

Fisher, T (1998) *Developing as a Teacher of Geography*; Cambridge: Chris Kington.

Book for all geography teachers – NQTs and practising professionals.

Frase, L E (1992) *Maximizing People Power in Schools: Motivating and Managing Teachers and Staff*; Newbury Park, California: Corwin.

An immensely useful, entertaining, description of effective and ineffective school management (in the USA), with ideas on burnout, observation of teachers, setting goals, and how to help and, if necessary, get rid of incompetent teachers. The philosophy is of practical, assertive, management. A taste of it is given by the advice that managers should as a matter of course give demonstration lessons, so that those whom they manage know what is expected. See also Frase, L E (1990) *School Management by Wandering Around*.

Fukuyama, F (1992) *The End of History and The Last Man*; London: Penguin.

Not the end of history (ie events – including the fall of the Berlin Wall, just after the original article was published), but the end of history, 'that is, history understood as a single, coherent, evolutionary process, when taking into account the experience of all peoples in all times' – as in Hegel and Marx. Liberal democracy is that end, the end of directional history.

Further Education Unit (1983) *Flexible Learning Opportunities*; London: FEU.

Flexible learning defined and applied.

Glauert, E (1996) *Tracking Significant Achievement in Primary Science*; London: Hodder.

One of a series of books tracking significant achievement – as for example Sainsbury (1996) on English. The approach demonstrated here seems to be the way ahead with some of the complexities of the National Curriculum: ie keeping track of pupils' most important achievements, not assessing every element of each of the ATs for every piece of work.

Gleick, J (1987) *Chaos: Making a New Science*; London: Sphere.

A popular book about chaos theory. Two principles of the theory are unpredictability (that greater knowledge doesn't necessarily lead to greater predictive powers) and the importance of physical causation (so change over time, for example change resulting from natural selection, must also mesh with simple physical causation). These principles might be applied to much history: accurate prediction is a sign of good history, and for all the grand theories of the 'direction' of history , there must still be real people making real things happen.

Grace, G (1995) *School Leadership: Beyond Education Management: An Essay in Policy Scholarship*; London: Falmer.

Part of the resurgence of leadership, rather than management, studies. Sensitive and well aware of the history of education management and leadership. Specialist work, too, on the dilemmas of Catholic Headteachers, and on women in educational leadership.

Griffin, J & Eddershaw, D (1994) *Using Local History Sources: A Teachers' Guide for the National Curriculum*; London: Hodder & Stoughton.

Aimed at KS1-3, conscious of the number of non-specialists teaching local history. Chapters on the whole range of local sources, from artefacts to school logbooks. The advice given is always qualified, including difficulties with the source, and there are always ICT references.

Halliday, F (1983, second edition 1986) *The Making of the Second Cold War*; London: Verso.

Excellent book (described on the back cover as 'the most authoritative, balanced and comprehensive account of the origins of the new phase of East-West tension'), yet deeply pessimistic about the Cold War, only three or four years before it ended. So, in the final pages of the book 'there seemed little prospect of a rapid end to the Cold War II ... This conflict is permanent and global'. Halliday does, though, mention that 'Hegel insisted that history is cunning, that human actions do not have the consequences that those who perform them intend'.

Haydn, T, Arthur, J, & Hunt, M (1997) *Learning to Teach History in the Secondary School: A Companion to School Experience*; London: Routledge.

All good stuff, designed for initial teacher trainees and useful for new and experienced teachers. Chapter 8 on ICT is most impressive, and uses the current government's wide definition of ICT – i.e. including radio, video, and so on, as well as computers.

Hinton, C (1990) *What is Evidence?*; London: John Murray.

An excellent book of and on evidence, rich with sources and questions on difficult issues such as bias and reliability. The book is pitched at GCSE level, but could be plundered for work at all levels.

Hodgson, N (1988) *Classroom Display: Improving the Visual Environment in Schools*; Diss: Tarquin.

Very clear, very fully illustrated, thorough guide to display from the smallest to the largest scale, for primary and secondary schools. Practical advice on, for example, lettering, layout and binding, as well as broader advice on raising the school's profile in the community.

Inman, S & Buck, M (eds) (1995) *Adding Value?: Schools' responsibility for pupils' personal development*; Stoke-on-Trent: Trentham.

A collection of articles on spirituality, citizenship, and so on, by reliable authors with a solid, even knowledge-based, thread running through it.

Jackson, J L (1994) *Share Our World: A Collection of Multi-Faith Fables for the Primary School Assembly*; Hemel Hempstead: Simon & Schuster.

Superb, readable, stories from all manner of traditions, religious and not, written in a style ideal for reading aloud. Designed for primary schools, but useable by absolutely everyone.

Jones, J (1994) *Teacher as Reflective Professional*; London: Institute of Education, Occasional Papers in Teacher Education and Training.

Work on reflective practice, out of Schön, etc, leading to PGCE portfolio work.

Jones, P & Sparks, N (1996) *Effective Heads of Department (The School Effectiveness Series)*; Stafford: Network Educational Press Ltd.

A useful tick-listing sort of book on teamwork, planning, monitoring/evaluating, and – to suit the series style – effective teaching and learning.

Kress, G & van Leeuwen, T (1990, second edition 1996) *Reading Images: The Grammar of Visual Design*.

Theory book, full of examples, by authors who have also written much on reading words.

Lane, P (1984, revised 1992) *Revise World History 1870–1992: A Complete Revision Course for GCSE*; London: Letts.

Good revision and teacher's aid. Interesting on the Communist Block, as it was first written in 1984 but revised up to 1992.

Lee, P, White, J, Walsh, P & Slater, J (1992) *The Aims of School History: The National Curriculum and Beyond*; London: Tufnell.

Good position statements by some key players.

Lewis, M & Wray, D (1996) *Writing Frames: Scaffolding Children's Non-Fiction Writing in a Range of Genres*; Reading: Reading and Language Information Centre.

A short but detailed book of framing templates for children to use when, designed for primary and lower secondary (including special needs) pupils. The scaffolding approach is justified in terms of Vygotsky, and is (happily) presented as one of many possible approaches.

Lunzer, E A & Gardner, K (eds) (1979) *The Effective Use of Reading*; London: Heinemann/Schools Council.

Major research project on reading across the curriculum. Clearly written, full of statistics, and with reliable if hesitant advice. Led to the later use of the term DART in the education world.

Lurie, A (1990) *Don't Tell the Grown-Ups: Subversive Children's Literature*; London: Bloomsbury.

A lovely book, giving such insight into the complex world of children's understanding and imagination. Interesting, too, for those who want to understand, or teach, controversial issues.

McAlpine, A, Brown, S, McIntyre, D, & Hagger, H (1988) *Student-Teachers Learning from Experienced Teachers*; Edinburgh: Scottish Council for Research in Education.

Joint work with Oxford University (presumably because of their mentor scheme). Good on simple methods of 'interviewing' teachers, to help them improve.

MacBeath, J & Turner, M (1990) *Learning out of School: Report of Research Study Carried out at Jordanhill College*; Glasgow: Jordanhill College.

Probably the central text on homework and how it is (or could/should) be approached, and research on the topic. The study was based on thirteen varied Scottish (primary & secondary) schools.

Macdonald, I, Bhavnani, R, Khan, L, & John, G (1989) *Murder in the Playground: The Report of the Macdonald Inquiry into Racism and Racial Violence in Manchester Schools*; London: Longsight Press.

A report, all the more shocking for its cool style, into a playground murder of an Asian boy by a white boy. The report is both into the incident and into more general issues, including the media coverage of the issue, the local and national political response, the history of anti-racist education, and broader educational issues such as empowerment.

Maddern, E (1992) *A Teacher's Guide to Storytelling at Historic Sites*; London: English Heritage.

Teachers should dare to tell stories. The book gives good advice and makes storytelling seem obvious and important.

Marland, M (1971) *Head of Department*; London: Heinemann.

Useful, sympathetic, non-dogmatic, guide.

Moon, B & Shelton Mayes, A (eds) (1994) *Teaching and Learning in the Secondary School*; London: Routledge/Open University.

An enormously action-packed set of articles, put together for the Open University's PGCE, but which will no doubt be used by many others.

Morgan, G (1986) *Images of Organization*; Thousand Oaks, California: Sage.

A masterly book on how organisations can be understood and described, combining originality and authority: an instant new standard text. Helpful for anyone wanting to understand the way a school, for example, works – with much guidance on organisational metaphors. Is the school one big happy family? An exam factory? Riven by class conflict?

National Council for Educational Technology (1990) *Developing Partnerships between Librarians and Teachers in Flexible Learning*; Coventry: NCET.

A well-produced pack, more a training manual than a 'position paper', which goes well beyond the rather narrow title, and should stimulate good discussion amongst all manner of teachers and their non-teaching colleagues.

National Curriculum Council (1991) *Teaching Talking and Learning in Key Stage Three: A booklet for teachers based on the work of the National Oracy Project*; York: NCC and National Oracy Project.

Many different techniques, on using talk and much more. Plenty on group work, gender, bilingualism, and everything else.

National Oracy Project (1991) *Assessment Through Talk in Key Stages 3 & 4: Occasional Papers in Oracy No. 4*; London: National Oracy Project.

Case studies of effective oral assessment. Useful for combating cynicism, and for getting simple ideas.

Nichol, J (1995) *Teaching History at Key Stage 3*; Cambridge: Chris Kington.

Chapter 1 covers key issues, including the need for action research by teachers (to be applied to pupils, too). Chapter 2 on the National Curriculum (post-Dearing). Chapter 3 on ICT. Ending with examples of worksheets.

Norman, K (ed) (1992) *Thinking Voices: The Work of the National Oracy Project*; London: London: Hodder & Stoughton.

Series of brief, useful, articles on talk in the classroom – covering practical and theoretical issues.

Office for Standards in Education (1995) *History: A Review of Inspection Findings 1993/94*; London: HMSO.

Review of history teaching, in the usual Ofsted style. Poor lessons 'were characterised by one or more of lack of clear purpose, over-emphasis on direction by the teacher with no opportunities for pupils to consolidate their knowledge, lack of differentiation and inappropriate resources and tasks. In too many lessons provision was insufficiently challenging, and did not build effectively on the existing capabilities of the pupils'.

Perfetti, C A, Britt, M A & Georgi, M C (1995) *Text-Based Learning and Reasoning: Studies in History*; Hillsdate, New Jersey: Lawrence Erlbaum Associates.

'To learn history is to learn a story. To understand history as a nonexpert is to know the story. There is more to both learning and understanding history than this, of course. We claim merely that what one knows includes a story.' The authors go on to investigate the relationship between stories and explanations, and much else besides. They include a chapter about learning and reasoning about controversy; and reasoning about hypothetical scenarios.

Peter, M (ed) (1992) *Differentiation: Ways Forward*; Stafford: National Association for Special Educational Needs. (Reprinted from the *British Journal of Special Education*, Volume 19, No. 1, March 1992.)

A clear and detailed book of guidance on varieties of differentiation, well aware of the complexities of teaching.

Powling, C (1997) *Storytelling in Schools ... And Some Stories About It*; Reading: Reading and Language Information Centre.

A good looking and friendly book of and about storytelling, that should convince any doubters of the joys of telling, and getting children to tell, stories. As Dickens is supposed to have said, 'Make them laugh, make them cry, make them ... wait'. Bruner talks of two modes of cognitive functioning, irreducible to one another – a well-formed argument, and a good story.

Pownall, J & Hutson, N (1992) *A Teacher's Guide to Science and the Historic Environment*; London: English Heritage.

Work on structures and on the environment, with good practical ideas for science teachers and for history teachers.

Pring, R & Walford, G (eds) (1997) *Affirming the Comprehensive Ideal*; London: Falmer.

A timely book, stressing the retrogade effects of the recent promotion of various forms of selection.

Purkis, S (1993) *A Teacher's Guide to Using School Buildings*; London: English Heritage.

Good work on buildings and also documents and photographs. Ideas on work in many subjects beyond history, too.

Roberts, W (1989) *Leadership Secrets of Attila the Hun*; London: Bantam Books.

Rather bizarre, compulsive, reconstruction of Attila's probable techniques, endlessly applicable – not least to teachers both in the classroom and the staffroom.

Rudduck, J, Chaplain, R, & Wallace, G (eds) (1996) *School Improvement: What Can Pupils Tell Us?*; London: Fulton.

A book for teachers and researchers alike. It should be no surprise to get a whole book on what pupils think about school, but it is. Throughout, the voices of the pupils are clear and perceptive. If the conclusions seem obvious – such as engage pupils as partners in school improvement, and listen even to the voices of the disengaged – they are still not heard in most other books on school improvement, and are overlooked by most schools.

Rush, C (1994) *Last Lesson of the Afternoon: A Satire*; Edinburgh: Canongate.

A novel incorporating a spectacularly cynical view of education, from the perspective of the charismatic, eccentric, teacher-as-guru, school of teaching. Critical of teacher training (as useless) and any systematic bureaucratic policy-based work in schools (as hypocritical, counter-productive and even evil).

Sainsbury, M (1996) *Tracking Significant Achievement in Primary English*; London: Hodder.

See Glauert, 1996.

Salmon, P (1985) *Living in Time: A New Look at Personal Development*; London: Dent.

A psychologist's work on stages and types of life, set in time, from young to old, with gender, loss and death along the way.

Schön, D A (1983) *The Reflective Practitioner;* New York: Basic Books

The classic text of reflective practice in the professions.

Schutz, A (1973) *Collected Papers 1: The Problem of Social Reality*; The Hague: Martinus Nijhoff.

The philosopher of 'multiple realities'.

Sebba, J (1994) *History for All*; London: Fulton.

One of a series for teachers of pupils with SEN, whether in special or mainstream schools. This one, as so many, would be good for teachers of all pupils.

Senge, P M (1990) *The Fifth Discipline*; Doubleday.

How to create 'learning organisations'. A happy management book, written not for schools, but for commercial organisations, yet applicable (and increasingly applied) to schools.

Shephard, C, Corbishley, M, Large, A, & Tames, R (1991) *Discovering the Past Y7: Contrasts & Connections*; London: John Murray.

The Roman, Medieval, and Islamic combined Schools History Project textbook for KS3. Big questions spread over several pages. Full of sources.

Slater, J (1995) *Teaching History in the New Europe*; London: Cassell/Council of Europe.

A good attempt, by a very reliable writer, to place history in the European Union, based on work throughout the EU. Good definitions of bias, prejudice, and indoctrination.

Spackman, F (1991) *Teachers' Professional Responsibilities*; London: Fulton/Roehampton Institute.

Brief practical guide to being a teacher (other than the teaching). Sensible advice in a legal framework.

Stern, L J (1994, 2nd edition 1997) *The Beginning Teacher as Researcher: A Guide for School Tutors*; London: Institute of Education, Occasional Papers in Teacher Education and Training.

Booklet for the Institute's PGCE course, also used to support all forms of research in schools.

Stern, L J (1995) *Learning to Teach: a Guide for School-based Initial and In-service Training*; London: Fulton.

A guide to teaching, schools and educational research for students, tutors and researcher-practitioners.

Stern, L J (1997) *Homework and Study Support: A Guide for Teachers and Parents*; London: Fulton.

A practical guide to homework, covering all the National Curriculum subjects and much more.

Stern, L J (1998) *Byting Back: Religious Education Sinks its Teeth into Computers: A Guide and In-Service Training Pack for RE Teachers*; Isleworth: BFSS National RE Centre.

A guide for RE teachers and those interested in using computers for personal and spiritual development, as well as for the accumulation of 'facts'. It includes an annotated version of the whole IT National Curriculum.

Stock, B (1991) *Health and Safety in Schools*; Kingston, Surrey: Croner.

Detailed, punchy, book, in the very reliable Croner series, on all aspects of safety law and good practice – including the issue of stress at work.

Strauss, A L & Corbin, J (1990) *Basics of Qualitative Research: Grounded Theory Procedures and Techniques*; London: Sage.

This book is a detailed guide to qualitative research methods. Qualitative analysis is defined as 'a nonmathematical analytical procedure that results in findings derived from data gathered by a variety of means'. It therefore covers most of the on-going learning done by teachers, even if quantitative data and analysis are more popular in formal research proposals.

Strobl, G (1997) 'Shakespeare and the Nazis'; in *History Today*, vol 47 (5) (May 1997) p 16–21.

An interesting look at the ways in which Shakespeare's plays were favoured by Nazi leaders, and ways in which they were, or could be, used subversively. The article also, of course, illuminates the uses of Shakespeare in the UK.

Taylor, J (1996) *Joseph Lancaster: The Poor Child's Friend: Educating the Poor in the Early Nineteenth Century*; West Wickham, Kent: Campanile Press.

A sympathetic account of the founder of the monitorial system. Lancaster's work and influence around the world, from the early 19th century, highlights the absurdity of narrow, inward-looking, curriculum and school developments popular with some in the late 20th century.

Tolley, H, Biddulph, M & Fisher, T (1996a) *Beginning Teaching Workbook 1: Pre-entry to Initial Teacher Training*; Cambridge: Chris Kington.

Tolley, H, Biddulph, M & Fisher, T (1996b) *Beginning Teaching Workbook 2: Beginning Initial Teacher Training*; Cambridge: Chris Kington.

Tolley, H, Biddulph, M & Fisher, T (1996c) *Beginning Teaching Workbook 3: Block Teaching Practice*; Cambridge: Chris Kington.

Tolley, H, Biddulph, M & Fisher, T (1996d) *Beginning Teaching Workbook 4: Pre-entry to First Teaching Post*; Cambridge: Chris Kington.

Tolley, H, Biddulph, M & Fisher, T (1996e) *Beginning Teaching Workbook 5: The First Year of Teaching*; Cambridge: Chris Kington.

Tolley, H, Biddulph, M & Fisher, T (1996f) *Beginning Teaching Workbook 6: Beyond the First Year of Teaching*; Cambridge: Chris Kington.

The series taking people through from the start of initial teacher education to RQT (recently qualified teacher) status. A philosophy of portfolios and reflective practice.

Topping, K (1988) *The Peer Tutoring Handbook: Promoting Co-operative Learning*; London: Croom Helm.

A practical guide for using, monitoring, and assessing peer tutoring in schools.

TVEI (1989) *TVEI Developments 10: Flexible Learning*; Sheffield: Training Agency.

A set of brief articles, describing good practice in flexible learning.

Watkins, C & Whalley, C (1993) *Mentoring: Resources for School-Based Development*; London: Kogan Page.

A practical workbook for mentors.

Watts, R & Grosvenor, I (eds) (1995) *Crossing the Key Stages of History: Effective History Teaching 5–16 and Beyond*; London: Fulton.

A coherent set of articles on planning history, sensitive to local variations, and to variations in perspective, culture, ethnicity, gender, writing, etc. It is important to plan across the key stages, in terms of pupils' rights to outline and in-depth history, and different perspectives.

Index

This index includes very few names of authors, as these are mostly listed alphabetically in the bibliography, and few references to 'history', as these would encompass the entire book.

art 42, 50, 83, 93, 94
artefacts 57, 59, 95
assessment 11, 14, 35, 64–77

boredom 35–36

CHATA (Concepts of History and Teaching Approaches) 68, 80
chronology 5, 25, 30–31, 64, 69, 71
competences (*see also* standards) 7–8
controversy 33, 94, 98
cross-curricular issues (*see also* equality of opportunity, ICT, language, PSMSC) 79, 81

differentiation 12, 37–45, 85, 98
directed activities related to texts (DART) 42–43, 52, 83, 93
display 33, 54, 57, 59, 96

English (*see* language, stories)
equality of opportunity 15, 41, 51, 79, 81, 83, 85, 94, 95, 97
evidence 7–9, 10, 14, 25, 33, 34, 96
expertise 38, 40, 87–89

group work 11, 12, 31, 33, 35, 38

history
   the nature of history 25, 48, 95, 98
   the purpose of history 23, 24, 26–27, 48, 97
homework 11, 12, 35–36, 43–46, 53, 59, 85, 97, 99
information and communication technology (ICT) 10, 12, 13, 41, 50–51, 81, 95, 96, 99
language 11, 13, 26, 38, 48–50, 52, 66, 69, 82–3, 84, 97, 98
leadership and management 41, 86, 88–91, 94, 96, 97
learning 37
   flexible learning 41, 96, 100
   learning by teachers (*see also* reflective practice) 13, 15, 22, 38, 93, 94
   learning organisation 22, 97, 99

learning theory (*see also* Vygotsky) 10, 24
legal issues 10, 15, 54, 55–7, 99
librarians 48, 98

mentoring 5, 9, 22, 40, 77, 79, 85, 92, 97, 100
music 42, 49–50

personal, social, moral, spiritual and cultural development (PSMSC) 11, 79–81, 96
planning 7, 8, 11, 18, 22, 25, 27, 29–36, 38, 39, 43, 44, 47, 48, 59, 61, 68, 69, 77, 85, 92, 100
presentations 33, 35–36
primary schools 5, 10, 23, 25, 26, 27, 44, 48, 59, 61, 63, 66, 82, 94, 95, 96, 100
professional development portfolio 22, 27, 100

questioning 35

reflective practice (*see also* learning by teachers) 8, 91, 96, 99, 100
research 22, 51, 92, 93, 99
resources 12, 42, 47–61, 93

Shakespeare 49, 100
song (*see* music)
special needs 11, 13, 38, 52, 83–85, 99
standards for the award of qualified teacher status (QTS) 7–8, 10–16, 17–21, 95
stories 48–50, 97, 98
stress 7, 29, 68, 92

target-setting 8–9, 17–21
team teaching 38–39
texts (*see also* language) 41–42, 47–50

visits 53, 54–59, 94, 98
Vygotsky 24, 40, 94

worksheets 51–53